12 *Mastering* RULES FOR LIFE

Tidy up your outer and inner disorder (Vol.4)

by

Kristina Harris

Table of Contents

Foreword

Rules? More rules? Really? Isn't life complicated enough, restricting enough, without abstract rules that don't take our unique, individual situations into account? And given that our brains are plastic, and all develop differently based on our life experiences, why even expect that a few rules might be helpful to us all?

People don't clamour for rules, even in the Bible … as when Moses comes down the mountain, after a long absence, bearing the tablets inscribed with ten commandments, and finds the Children of Israel in revelry. They'd been Pharaoh's slaves and subject to his tyrannical regulations for four hundred years, and after that Moses subjected them to the harsh desert wilderness for another forty years, to purify them of their slavishness. Now, free at last, they are unbridled, and have lost all control as they dance wildly around an idol, a golden calf, displaying all manner of corporeal corruption.

"I've got some good news … and I've got some bad news," the lawgiver yells to them. "Which do you want first?"

"The good news!" the hedonists reply.

"I got Him from fifteen commandments down to ten!"

"Hallelujah!" cries the unruly crowd. "And the bad?"

"Adultery is still in."

So rules there will be—but, please, not too many. We are ambivalent about rules, even when we know they are good for us. If we are spirited souls, if we have character, rules seem restrictive, an affront to our sense of agency and our pride in working out our own lives. Why should we be judged according to another's rule?

And judged we are. After all, God didn't give Moses "The Ten Suggestions," he gave Commandments; and if I'm a free agent, my first reaction to a command might just be that nobody, not even God, tells me what to do, even if it's good for me. But the story of the golden calf also reminds us that without rules we quickly become slaves to our passions—and there's nothing freeing about that.

And the story suggests something more: unchaperoned, and left to our own untutored judgment, we are quick to aim low and worship qualities that are beneath us—in this case, an artificial animal that brings out our own animal instincts in a completely unregulated way. The old Hebrew story makes it clear how the ancients felt about our prospects for civilized behaviour in the absence of rules that seek to elevate our gaze and raise our standards.

One neat thing about the Bible story is that it doesn't simply list its rules, as lawyers or legislators or administrators might; it embeds them in a dramatic tale that illustrates why we need them, thereby making them easier to understand. Similarly, in this book Professor Peterson doesn't just propose his twelve rules, he tells stories, too, bringing to bear his knowledge of many fields as he illustrates and explains why the best rules do not ultimately restrict us but instead facilitate our goals and make for fuller, freer lives.

The first time I met Jordan Peterson was on September 12, 2004, at the home of two mutual friends, TV producer Wodek Szemberg and medical internist Estera Bekier. It was Wodek's birthday party. Wodek and Estera are Polish émigrés who grew up within the Soviet empire, where it was understood that many topics were off limits, and that casually questioning certain social arrangements and philosophical ideas (not to mention the regime itself) could mean big trouble.

But now, host and hostess luxuriated in easygoing, honest talk, by having elegant parties devoted to the pleasure of saying what you *really* thought and hearing others do the same, in an uninhibited give-and-take. Here, the rule was "Speak your mind." If the conversation turned to politics, people of different political persuasions spoke to each other—indeed, looked forward to it—in a manner that is increasingly rare. Sometimes Wodek's own opinions, or truths, exploded out of him, as did his laugh. Then he'd hug whoever had made him laugh or provoked him to speak his mind with greater intensity than even he might have intended. This was the best part of the parties, and this frankness, and his warm embraces, made it worth provoking him. Meanwhile, Estera's voice lilted across the room on a very precise path towards its intended listener. Truth explosions didn't make the atmosphere any less easygoing for the company—they made for more truth explosions!—

liberating us, and more laughs, and making the whole evening more pleasant, because with de-repressing Eastern Europeans like the Szemberg-Bekiers, you always knew with what and with whom you were dealing, and that frankness was enlivening. Honoré de Balzac, the novelist, once described the balls and parties in his native France, observing that what appeared to be a single party was always really two. In the first hours, the gathering was suffused with bored people posing and posturing, and attendees who came to meet perhaps one special person who would confirm them in their beauty and status. Then, only in the very late hours, after most of the guests had left, would the second party, the real party, begin. Here the conversation was shared by each person present, and open-hearted laughter replaced the starchy airs. At Estera and Wodek's parties, this kind of wee-hours-of-the-morning disclosure and intimacy often began as soon as we entered the room.

Wodek is a silver-haired, lion-maned hunter, always on the lookout for potential public intellectuals, who knows how to spot people who can *really* talk in front of a TV camera and who look authentic because they are (the camera picks up on that). He often invites such people to these salons. That day Wodek brought a psychology professor, from my own University of Toronto, who fit the bill: intellect and emotion in tandem. Wodek was the first to put Jordan Peterson in front of a camera, and thought of him as a teacher in search of students—because he was always ready to explain. And it helped that he liked the camera and that the camera liked him back.

That afternoon there was a large table set outside in the Szemberg-Bekiers' garden; around it was gathered the usual collection of lips and ears, and loquacious virtuosos. We seemed, however, to be plagued by a buzzing paparazzi of bees, and here was this new fellow at the table, with an Albertan accent, in cowboy boots, who was ignoring them, and kept on talking. He kept talking while the rest of us were playing musical chairs to keep away from the pests, yet also trying to remain at the table because this new addition to our gatherings was so interesting.

He had this odd habit of speaking about the deepest questions to whoever was at this table—most of them new acquaintances—as though he were just making small talk. Or, if he did do small talk, the interval between "How do you know Wodek and Estera?" or "I was a beekeeper once, so I'm used to them" and more serious topics would be nanoseconds.

One might hear such questions discussed at parties where professors and professionals gather, but usually the conversation would remain between two specialists in the topic, off in a corner, or if shared with the whole group it was often not without someone preening. But this Peterson, though erudite, didn't come across as a pedant. He had the enthusiasm of a kid who had just learned something new and had to share it. He seemed to be assuming, as a child would—before learning how dulled adults can become—that if he thought something was interesting, then so might others. There was something boyish in the cowboy, in his broaching of subjects as though we had all grown up together in the same small town, or family, and had all been thinking about the very same problems of human existence all along.

Peterson wasn't really an "eccentric"; he had sufficient conventional chops, had been a Harvard professor, was a gentleman (as cowboys can be) though he did say *damn* and *bloody* a lot, in a rural 1950s sort of way. But everyone listened, with fascination on their faces, because he was in fact addressing questions of concern to everyone at the table.

There was something freeing about being with a person so learned yet speaking in such an unedited way. His thinking was motoric; it seemed he needed to think *aloud*, to use his motor cortex to think, but that motor also had to run fast to work properly. To get to liftoff. Not quite manic, but his idling speed revved high. Spirited thoughts were tumbling out. But unlike many academics who take the floor and hold it, if someone challenged or corrected him he really seemed to *like* it. He didn't rear up and neigh. He'd say, in a kind of folksy way, "Yeah," and bow his head involuntarily, wag it if he had overlooked something, laughing at himself for overgeneralizing. He appreciated being shown another side of an issue, and it became clear that thinking through a problem was, for him, a dialogic process.

One could not but be struck by another unusual thing about him: for an egghead Peterson was extremely practical. His examples were filled with applications to everyday life: business management, how to make furniture (he made much of his own), designing a simple house, making a room beautiful (now an internet meme) or in another, specific case related to education, creating an online writing project that kept minority students from dropping out of school by getting them to do a kind of psychoanalytic exercise on themselves, in which they would free-associate about their past, present and future (now known as the Self-Authoring Program).

I was always especially fond of mid-Western, Prairie types who come from a farm (where they learned all about nature), or from a very small town, and who have worked with their hands to make things, spent long periods outside in the harsh elements, and are often self-educated and go to university against the odds. I found them quite unlike their sophisticated but somewhat denatured urban counterparts, for whom higher education was pre-ordained, and for that reason sometimes taken for granted, or thought of not as an end in itself but simply as a life stage in the service of career advancement. These Westerners were different: self-made, unentitled, hands on, neighbourly and less precious than many of their big-city peers, who increasingly spend their lives indoors, manipulating symbols on computers. This cowboy psychologist seemed to care about a thought only if it might, in some way, be helpful to someone.

We became friends. As a psychiatrist and psychoanalyst who loves literature, I was drawn to him because here was a clinician who also had given himself a great books education, and who not only loved soulful Russian novels, philosophy and ancient mythology, but who also seemed to treat them as his most treasured inheritance. But he also did illuminating statistical research on personality and temperament, and had studied neuroscience. Though trained as a behaviourist, he was powerfully drawn to psychoanalysis with its focus on dreams, archetypes, the persistence of childhood conflicts in the adult, and the role of defences and rationalization in everyday life. He was also an outlier in being the only member of the research-oriented Department of Psychology at the University of Toronto who also kept a clinical practice.

On my visits, our conversations began with banter and laughter—that was the small-town Peterson from the Alberta hinterland—his teenage years right out of the movie *FUBAR*—welcoming you into his home. The house had been gutted by Tammy, his wife, and himself, and turned into perhaps the most fascinating and shocking middle-class home I had seen. They had art, some carved masks, and abstract portraits, but they were overwhelmed by a huge collection of original Socialist Realist paintings of Lenin and the early Communists commissioned by the USSR. Not long after the Soviet Union fell, and most of the world breathed a sigh of relief, Peterson began purchasing this propaganda for a song online. Paintings lionizing the Soviet revolutionary spirit completely filled every single wall, the ceilings, even the bathrooms. The paintings were not there because Jordan had any totalitarian sympathies, but because he wanted to remind himself of something he knew he and everyone would rather forget: that hundreds of millions were murdered in the name of utopia.

It took getting used to, this semi-haunted house "decorated" by a delusion that had practically destroyed mankind. But it was eased by his wonderful and unique spouse, Tammy, who was all in, who embraced and encouraged this unusual need for expression! These paintings provided a visitor with the first window onto the full extent of Jordan's concern about our human capacity for evil in the name of good, and the psychological mystery of self-deception (how can a person deceive himself and get away with it?)—an interest we share. And then there were also the hours we'd spend discussing what I might call a lesser problem (lesser because rarer), the human capacity for evil for the sake of evil, the joy some people take in destroying others, captured famously by the seventeenth-century English poet John Milton in *Paradise Lost.*

And so we'd chat and have our tea in his kitchen-underworld, walled by this odd art collection, a visual marker of his earnest quest to move beyond simplistic ideology, left or right, and not repeat mistakes of the past. After a while, there was nothing peculiar about taking tea in the kitchen, discussing family issues, one's latest reading, with those ominous pictures hovering. It was just living in the world as it was, or in some places, is.

In Jordan's first and only book before this one, *Maps of Meaning,* he shares his profound insights into universal themes of world mythology, and explains how all cultures have created stories to help us grapple with, and ultimately map, the chaos into which we are thrown at birth; this chaos is everything that is unknown to us, and any unexplored territory that we must traverse, be it in the world outside or the psyche within.

Combining evolution, the neuroscience of emotion, some of the best of Jung, some of Freud, much of the great works of Nietzsche, Dostoevsky, Solzhenitsyn, Eliade, Neumann, Piaget, Frye and Frankl, *Maps of Meaning,* published nearly two decades ago, shows Jordan's wide-ranging approach to understanding how human beings and the human brain deal with the archetypal situation that arises whenever we, in our daily lives, must face something we do not understand. The brilliance of the book is in his demonstration of how rooted this situation is in evolution, our DNA, our brains and our most ancient stories. And he shows that these stories have survived because they still provide guidance in dealing with uncertainty, and the unavoidable unknown.

One of the many virtues of the book you are reading now is that it provides an entry point into *Maps of Meaning*, which is a highly complex work because Jordan was working out his approach to psychology as he wrote it. But it was foundational, because no matter how different our genes or life experiences may be, or how differently our plastic brains are wired by our experience, we all have to deal with the unknown, and we all attempt to move from chaos to order. And this is why many of the rules in this book, being based on *Maps of Meaning*, have an element of universality to them.

Maps of Meaning was sparked by Jordan's agonized awareness, as a teenager growing up in the midst of the Cold War, that much of mankind seemed on the verge of blowing up the planet to defend their various identities. He felt he had to understand how it could be that people would sacrifice everything for an "identity," whatever that was. And he felt he had to understand the ideologies that drove totalitarian regimes to a variant of that same behaviour: killing their own citizens. In *Maps of Meaning*, and again in this book, one of the matters he cautions readers to be most wary of is ideology, no matter who is peddling it or to what end.

Ideologies are simple ideas, disguised as science or philosophy, that purport to explain the complexity of the world and offer remedies that will perfect it. Ideologues are people who pretend they know how to "make the world a better place" before they've taken care of their own chaos within. (The warrior identity that their ideology gives them covers over that chaos.) That's hubris, of course, and one of the most important themes of this book, is "set your house in order" first, and Jordan provides practical advice on how to do this.

Ideologies are substitutes for true knowledge, and ideologues are always dangerous when they come to power, because a simple-minded I-know-it-all approach is no match for the complexity of existence. Furthermore, when their social contraptions fail to fly, ideologues blame not themselves but all who see through the simplifications. Another great U of T professor, Lewis Feuer, in his book *Ideology and the Ideologists*, observed that ideologies retool the very religious stories they purport to have supplanted, but eliminate the narrative and psychological richness. Communism borrowed from the story of the Children of Israel in Egypt, with an enslaved class, rich persecutors, a leader, like Lenin, who goes abroad, lives among the enslavers, and then leads the enslaved to the promised land (the utopia; the dictatorship of the proletariat).

To understand ideology, Jordan read extensively about not only the Soviet gulag, but also the Holocaust and the rise of Nazism. I had never before met a person, born Christian and of my generation, who was so utterly tormented by what happened in Europe to the Jews, and who had worked so hard to understand how it could have occurred. I too had studied this in depth. My own father survived Auschwitz. My grandmother was middle-aged when she stood face to face with Dr. Josef Mengele, the Nazi physician who conducted unspeakably cruel experiments on his victims, and she survived Auschwitz by disobeying his order to join the line with the elderly, the grey and the weak, and instead slipping into a line with younger people. She avoided the gas chambers a second time by trading food for hair dye so she wouldn't be murdered for looking too old. My grandfather, her husband, survived the Mauthausen concentration camp, but choked to death on the first piece of solid food he was given, just before liberation day. I relate this, because years after we became friends, when Jordan would take a classical liberal stand for free speech, he would be accused by left-wing extremists as being a right-wing bigot.

Let me say, with all the moderation I can summon: *at best,* those accusers have simply not done their due diligence. I have; with a family history such as mine, one develops not only radar, but underwater sonar for right-wing bigotry; but even more important, one learns to recognize the kind of person with the comprehension, tools, good will and courage to combat it, and Jordan Peterson is *that* person.

My own dissatisfaction with modern political science's attempts to understand the rise of Nazism, totalitarianism and prejudice was a major factor in my decision to supplement my studies of political science with the study of the unconscious, projection, psychoanalysis, the regressive potential of group psychology, psychiatry and the brain. Jordan switched out of political science for similar reasons. With these important parallel interests, we didn't always agree on "the answers" (thank God), but we almost always agreed on the questions.

Our friendship wasn't all doom and gloom. I have made a habit of attending my fellow professors' classes at our university, and so attended his, which were always packed, and I saw what now millions have seen online: a brilliant, often dazzling public speaker who was at his best riffing like a jazz artist; at times he resembled an ardent Prairie preacher (not in evangelizing, but in his passion, in his ability to tell stories that convey the life-stakes that go with believing or disbelieving various ideas). Then he'd just as easily switch to do a breathtakingly systematic summary of a series of scientific studies. He was a master at helping students become more reflective, and take themselves and their futures seriously. He taught them to respect many of the greatest books ever written. He gave vivid examples from clinical practice, was (appropriately) self-revealing, even of his own vulnerabilities, and made fascinating links between evolution, the brain and religious stories. In a world where students are taught to see evolution and religion as simply opposed (by thinkers like Richard Dawkins), Jordan showed his students how evolution, of all things, helps to explain the profound psychological appeal and wisdom of many ancient stories, from Gilgamesh to the life of the Buddha, Egyptian mythology and the Bible. He showed, for instance, how stories about journeying voluntarily into the unknown—the hero's quest—mirror universal tasks for which the brain evolved. He respected the stories, was not reductionist, and never claimed to exhaust their wisdom. If he discussed a topic such as prejudice, or its emotional relatives fear and disgust, or the differences between the sexes on average, he was able to show how these traits evolved and why they survived.

Above all, he alerted his students to topics rarely discussed in university, such as the simple fact that all the ancients, from Buddha to the biblical authors, knew what every slightly worn-out adult knows, that life is suffering. If you are suffering, or someone close to you is, that's sad. But alas, it's not particularly special. We don't suffer only because "politicians are dimwitted," or "the system is corrupt," or because you and I, like almost everyone else, can *legitimately* describe ourselves, in some way, as a victim of something or someone. It is because we are born human that we are guaranteed a good dose of suffering. And chances are, if you or someone you love is not suffering now, they will be within five years, unless you are freakishly lucky. Rearing kids is hard, work is hard, aging, sickness and death are hard, and Jordan emphasized that doing all that totally on your own, without the benefit of a loving relationship, or wisdom, or the psychological insights of the greatest psychologists, only makes it harder. He wasn't scaring the students; in fact, they found this frank talk reassuring, because in the depths of their psyches, most of them knew what he said was true, even if there was never a forum to discuss it—perhaps because the adults in their lives had become so naively overprotective that they deluded themselves into thinking that not talking about suffering would in some way magically protect their children from it.

Here he would relate the myth of the hero, a cross-cultural theme explored psychoanalytically by Otto Rank, who noted, following Freud, that hero myths are similar in many cultures, a theme that was picked up by Carl Jung, Joseph Campbell and Erich Neumann, among others. Where Freud made great contributions in explaining neuroses by, among other things, focusing on understanding what we might call a failed-hero story (that of Oedipus), Jordan focused on triumphant heroes. In all these triumph stories, the hero has to go into the unknown, into an unexplored territory, and deal with a new great challenge and take great risks. In the process, something of himself has to die, or be given up, so he can be reborn and meet the challenge. This requires courage, something rarely discussed in a psychology class or textbook. During his recent public stand for free speech and against what I call "forced speech" (because it involves a government forcing citizens to voice political views), the stakes were very high; he had much to lose, and knew it. Nonetheless, I saw him (and Tammy, for that matter) not only display such courage, but also continue to live by many of the rules in this book, some of which can be very demanding.

I saw him grow, from the remarkable person he was, into someone even more able and assured—through living by these rules. In fact, it was the process of writing this book, and developing these rules, that led him to take the stand he did against forced or compelled speech. And that is why, during those events, he started posting some of his thoughts about life and these rules on the internet. Now, over 100 million YouTube hits later, we know they have struck a chord.

Given our distaste for rules, how do we explain the extraordinary response to his lectures, which give rules? In Jordan's case, it was of course his charisma and a rare willingness to stand for a principle that got him a wide hearing online initially; views of his first YouTube statements quickly numbered in the hundreds of thousands. But people have kept listening because what he is saying meets a deep and unarticulated need. And that is because alongside our wish to be free of rules, we all search for structure.

The hunger among many younger people for rules, or at least guidelines, is greater today for good reason. In the West at least, millennials are living through a unique historical situation. They are, I believe, the first generation to have been so thoroughly taught two seemingly contradictory ideas about morality, simultaneously—at their schools, colleges and universities, by many in my own generation. This contradiction has left them at times disoriented and uncertain, without guidance and, more tragically, deprived of riches they don't even know exist.

The first idea or teaching is that morality is relative, at best a personal "value judgment." *Relative* means that there is no absolute right or wrong in anything; instead, morality and the rules associated with it are just a matter of personal opinion or happenstance, "relative to" or "related to" a particular framework, such as one's ethnicity, one's upbringing, or the culture or historical moment one is born into. It's nothing but an accident of birth. According to this argument (now a creed), history teaches that religions, tribes, nations and ethnic groups tend to disagree about fundamental matters, and always have. Today, the postmodernist left makes the additional claim that one group's morality is *nothing but* its attempt to exercise power over another group. So, the decent thing to do—once it becomes apparent how arbitrary your, and your society's, "moral values" are—is to show tolerance for people who think differently, and who come from different (diverse) backgrounds. That emphasis on tolerance is so paramount that for many people one of the worst character flaws a person can have is to be "judgmental."[fn1] And, since we don't know right from wrong, or what is good, just about *the most inappropriate thing an adult can do is give a young person advice* about how to live.

And so a generation has been raised untutored in what was once called, aptly, "practical wisdom," which guided previous generations. Millennials, often told they have received the finest education available anywhere, have actually suffered a form of serious intellectual and moral neglect. The relativists of my generation and Jordan's, many of whom became their professors, chose to devalue thousands of years of human knowledge about how to acquire virtue, dismissing it as passé, "not relevant" or even "oppressive." They were so successful at it that the very word "virtue" sounds out of date, and someone using it appears anachronistically moralistic and self-righteous.

The study of virtue is not quite the same as the study of morals (right and wrong, good and evil). Aristotle defined the virtues simply as the ways of behaving that are most conducive to happiness in life. Vice was defined as the ways of behaving least conducive to happiness. He observed that the virtues always aim for balance and avoid the extremes of the vices. Aristotle studied the virtues and the vices in his *Nicomachean Ethics.* It was a book based on experience and observation, not conjecture, about the kind of happiness that was possible for human beings. Cultivating *judgment* about the difference between virtue and vice is the beginning of wisdom, something that can never be out of date.

By contrast, our modern relativism begins by asserting that making judgments about how to live is impossible, because there is no *real* good, and no *true* virtue (as these too are relative). Thus relativism's closest approximation to "virtue" is "tolerance." Only tolerance will provide social cohesion between different groups, and save us from harming each other. On Facebook and other forms of social media, therefore, you signal your so-called virtue, telling everyone how tolerant, open and compassionate you are, and wait for likes to accumulate. (Leave aside that telling people you're virtuous isn't a virtue, it's self-promotion. Virtue signalling is not virtue. Virtue signalling is, quite possibly, our commonest vice.)

Intolerance of others' views (no matter how ignorant or incoherent they may be) is not simply wrong; in a world where there is no right or wrong, it is worse: it is a sign you are embarrassingly unsophisticated or, possibly, dangerous.

But it turns out that many people cannot tolerate the vacuum—the chaos—which is inherent in life, but made worse by this moral relativism; they cannot live without a moral compass, without an ideal at which to aim in their lives. (For relativists, ideals are values too, and like all values, they are merely "relative" and hardly worth sacrificing for.) So, right alongside relativism, we find the spread of nihilism and despair, and also the opposite of moral relativism: the blind certainty offered by ideologies that claim to have an answer for everything.

And so we arrive at the second teaching that millennials have been bombarded with. They sign up for a humanities course, to study greatest books ever written. But they're not assigned the books; instead they are given ideological attacks on them, based on some appalling simplification. Where the relativist is filled with uncertainty, the ideologue is the very opposite. He or she is hyper-judgmental and censorious, always knows what's wrong about others, and what to do about it. Sometimes it seems the only people willing to give advice in a relativistic society are those with the least to offer.

Modern moral relativism has many sources. As we in the West learned more history, we understood that different epochs had different moral codes. As we travelled the seas and explored the globe, we learned of far-flung tribes on different continents whose different moral codes made sense relative to, or within the framework of, their societies. Science played a role, too, by attacking the religious view of the world, and thus undermining the religious grounds for ethics and rules. Materialist social science implied that we could divide the world into facts (which all could observe, and were objective and "real") and values (which were subjective and personal). Then we could first agree on the facts, and, maybe, one day, develop a scientific code of ethics (which has yet to arrive). Moreover, by implying that values had a lesser reality than facts, science contributed in yet another way to moral relativism, for it treated "value" as secondary. (But the idea that we can easily separate facts and values was and remains naive; to some extent, one's values determine what one will pay attention to, and what will count as a fact.)

The idea that different societies had different rules and morals was known to the ancient world too, and it is interesting to compare its response to this realization with the modern response (relativism, nihilism and ideology). When the ancient Greeks sailed to India and elsewhere, they too discovered that rules, morals and customs differed from place to place, and saw that the explanation for what was right and wrong was often rooted in some ancestral authority. The Greek response was not despair, but a new invention: philosophy.

Socrates, reacting to the uncertainty bred by awareness of these conflicting moral codes, decided that instead of becoming a nihilist, a relativist or an ideologue, he would devote his life to the search for wisdom that could reason about these differences, i.e., he helped invent philosophy. He spent his life asking perplexing, foundational questions, such as "What is virtue?" and "How can one live the good life?" and "What is justice?" and he looked at different approaches, asking which seemed most coherent and most in accord with human nature. These are the kinds of questions that I believe animate this book.

For the ancients, the discovery that different people have different ideas about how, practically, to live, did not paralyze them; it deepened their understanding of humanity and led to some of the most satisfying conversations human beings have ever had, about how life might be lived.

Likewise, Aristotle. Instead of despairing about these differences in moral codes, Aristotle argued that though specific rules, laws and customs differed from place to place, what does not differ is that in all places human beings, by their nature, have a proclivity to make rules, laws and customs. To put this in modern terms, it seems that all human beings are, by some kind of biological endowment, so ineradicably concerned with morality that we create a structure of laws and rules wherever we are. The idea that human life can be free of moral concerns is a fantasy.

We are rule generators. And given that we are moral animals, what must be the effect of our simplistic modern relativism upon us? It means we are hobbling ourselves by pretending to be something we are not. It is a mask, but a strange one, for it mostly deceives the one who wears it. *Sccccratccch* the most clever postmodern-relativist professor's Mercedes with a key, and you will see how fast the mask of relativism (with its pretense that there can be neither right nor wrong) and the cloak of radical tolerance come off.

Because we do not yet have an ethics based on modern science, Jordan is not trying to develop his rules by wiping the slate clean—by dismissing thousands of years of wisdom as mere superstition and ignoring our greatest moral achievements. Far better to integrate the best of what we are now learning with the books human beings saw fit to preserve over millennia, and with the stories that have survived, against all odds, time's tendency to obliterate.

He is doing what reasonable guides have always done: he makes no claim that human wisdom begins with himself, but, rather, turns first to his own guides. And although the topics in this book are serious, Jordan often has great fun addressing them with a light touch, as the chapter headings convey. He makes no claim to be exhaustive, and sometimes the chapters consist of wide-ranging discussions of our psychology as he understands it.

So why not call this a book of "guidelines," a far more relaxed, user-friendly and less rigid sounding term than "rules"?

Because these really are rules. And the foremost rule is that you must take responsibility for your own life. Period.

One might think that a generation that has heard endlessly, from their more ideological teachers, about the rights, rights, rights that belong to them, would object to being told that they would do better to focus instead on taking responsibility. Yet this generation, many of whom were raised in small families by hyper-protective parents, on soft-surface playgrounds, and then taught in universities with "safe spaces" where they don't have to hear things they don't want to—schooled to be risk-averse—has among it, now, millions who feel stultified by this underestimation of their potential resilience and who have embraced Jordan's message that each individual has ultimate responsibility to bear; that if one wants to live a full life, one first sets one's own house in order; and only then can one sensibly aim to take on bigger responsibilities. The extent of this reaction has often moved both of us to the brink of tears.

Sometimes these rules are demanding. They require you to undertake an incremental process that over time will stretch you to a new limit. That requires, as I've said, venturing into the unknown. Stretching yourself beyond the boundaries of your current self requires carefully choosing and then pursuing ideals: ideals that are up there, above you, superior to you—and that you can't always be sure you will reach.

But if it's uncertain that our ideals are attainable, why do we bother reaching in the first place? Because if you don't reach for them, it is certain you will never feel that your life has meaning.

And perhaps because, as unfamiliar and strange as it sounds, in the deepest

Overture

This book has a short history and a long history. We'll begin with the short history.

In 2012, I started contributing to a website called Quora. On Quora, anyone can ask a question, of any sort—and anyone can answer. Readers upvote those answers they like, and downvote those they don't. In this manner, the most useful answers rise to the top, while the others sink into oblivion. I was curious about the site. I liked its free-for-all nature. The discussion was often compelling, and it was interesting to see the diverse range of opinions generated by the same question.

When I was taking a break (or avoiding work), I often turned to Quora, looking for questions to engage with. I considered, and eventually answered, such questions as "What's the difference between being happy and being content?", "What things get better as you age?" and "What makes life more meaningful?"

Quora tells you how many people have viewed your answer and how many upvotes you received. Thus, you can determine your reach, and see what people think of your ideas. Only a small minority of those who view an answer upvote it. As of July 2017, as I write this—and five years after I addressed "What makes life more meaningful?"—my answer to that question has received a relatively small audience (14,000 views, and 133 upvotes), while my response to the question about aging has been viewed by 7,200 people and received 36 upvotes. Not exactly home runs. However, it's to be expected. On such sites, most answers receive very little attention, while a tiny minority become disproportionately popular.

Soon after, I answered another question: "What are the most valuable things everyone should know?" I wrote a list of rules, or maxims; some dead serious, some tongue-in-cheek—"Be grateful in spite of your suffering," "Do not do things that you hate," "Do not hide things in the fog," and so on. The

Quora readers appeared pleased with this list. They commented on and shared it. They said such things as "I'm definitely printing this list out and keeping it as a reference. Simply phenomenal," and "You win Quora. We can just close the site now." Students at the University of Toronto, where I teach, came up to me and told me how much they liked it. To date, my answer to "What are the most valuable things …" has been viewed by a hundred and twenty thousand people and been upvoted twenty-three hundred times. Only a few hundred of the roughly six hundred thousand questions on Quora have cracked the two-thousand-upvote barrier. My procrastination-induced musings hit a nerve. I had written a 99.9 percentile answer.

It was not obvious to me when I wrote the list of rules for living that it was going to perform so well. I had put a fair bit of care into all the sixty or so answers I submitted in the few months surrounding that post. Nonetheless, Quora provides market research at its finest. The respondents are anonymous. They're disinterested, in the best sense. Their opinions are spontaneous and unbiased. So, I paid attention to the results, and thought about the reasons for that answer's disproportionate success. Perhaps I struck the right balance between the familiar and the unfamiliar while formulating the rules. Perhaps people were drawn to the structure that such rules imply. Perhaps people just like lists.

A few months earlier, in March of 2012, I had received an email from a literary agent. She had heard me speak on CBC radio during a show entitled *Just Say No to Happiness*, where I had criticized the idea that happiness was the proper goal for life. Over the previous decades I had read more than my share of dark books about the twentieth century, focusing particularly on Nazi Germany and the Soviet Union. Aleksandr Solzhenitsyn, the great documenter of the slave-labour-camp horrors of the latter, once wrote that the "pitiful ideology" holding that "human beings are created for happiness" was an ideology "done in by the first blow of the work assigner's cudgel."[1] In a crisis, the inevitable suffering that life entails can rapidly make a mockery of the idea that happiness is the proper pursuit of the individual. On the radio show, I suggested, instead, that a deeper meaning was required. I noted that the nature of such meaning was constantly re-presented in the great stories of the past, and that it had more to do with developing character in the face of suffering than with happiness. This is part of the long history of the present work.

From 1985 until 1999 I worked for about three hours a day on the only other book I have ever published: *Maps of Meaning: The Architecture of Belief.* During that time, and in the years since, I also taught a course on the material in that book, first at Harvard, and now at the University of Toronto. In 2013, observing the rise of YouTube, and because of the popularity of some work I had done with TVO, a Canadian public TV station, I decided to film my university and public lectures and place them online. They attracted an increasingly large audience—more than a million views by April 2016. The number of views has risen very dramatically since then (up to eighteen million as I write this), but that is in part because I became embroiled in a political controversy that drew an inordinate amount of attention.

That's another story. Maybe even another book.

I proposed in *Maps of Meaning* that the great myths and religious stories of the past, particularly those derived from an earlier, oral tradition, were *moral* in their intent, rather than descriptive. Thus, they did not concern themselves with what the world was, as a scientist might have it, but with how a human being should act. I suggested that our ancestors portrayed the world as a stage —a drama—instead of a place of objects. I described how I had come to believe that the constituent elements of the world as drama were order and chaos, and not material things.

Order is where the people around you act according to well-understood social norms, and remain predictable and cooperative. It's the world of social structure, explored territory, and familiarity. The state of Order is typically portrayed, symbolically—imaginatively—as masculine. It's the Wise King and the Tyrant, forever bound together, as society is simultaneously structure and oppression.

Chaos, by contrast, is where—or when—something unexpected happens. Chaos emerges, in trivial form, when you tell a joke at a party with people you think you know and a silent and embarrassing chill falls over the gathering. Chaos is what emerges more catastrophically when you suddenly find yourself without employment, or are betrayed by a lover. As the antithesis of symbolically masculine order, it's presented imaginatively as feminine. It's the new and unpredictable suddenly emerging in the midst of the commonplace familiar. It's Creation and Destruction, the source of new things and the destination of the dead (as nature, as opposed to culture, is simultaneously birth and demise).

Order and chaos are the yang and yin of the famous Taoist symbol: two serpents, head to tail. [fn1] Order is the white, masculine serpent; Chaos, its black, feminine counterpart. The black dot in the white—and the white in the black—indicate the possibility of transformation: just when things seem secure, the unknown can loom, unexpectedly and large. Conversely, just when everything seems lost, new order can emerge from catastrophe and chaos.

For the Taoists, meaning is to be found on the border between the ever-entwined pair. To walk that border is to stay on the path of life, the divine Way.

And that's much better than happiness.

The literary agent I referred to listened to the CBC radio broadcast where I discussed such issues. It left her asking herself deeper questions. She emailed me, asking if I had considered writing a book for a general audience. I had previously attempted to produce a more accessible version of *Maps of Meaning,* which is a very dense book. But I found that the spirit was neither in me during that attempt nor in the resultant manuscript. I think this was because I was imitating my former self, and my previous book, instead of occupying the place between order and chaos and producing something new. I suggested that she watch four of the lectures I had done for a TVO program called *Big Ideas* on my YouTube channel. I thought if she did that we could have a more informed and thorough discussion about what kind of topics I might address in a more publicly accessible book.

She contacted me a few weeks later, after watching all four lectures and discussing them with a colleague. Her interest had been further heightened, as had her commitment to the project. That was promising—and unexpected. I'm always surprised when people respond positively to what I am saying, given its seriousness and strange nature. I'm amazed I have been allowed (even encouraged) to teach what I taught first in Boston and now in Toronto. I've always thought that if people really noticed what I was teaching there would be Hell to pay. You can decide for yourself what truth there might be in that concern after reading this book. :)

She suggested that I write a guide of sorts to what a person needs "to live well"—whatever that might mean. I thought immediately about my Quora list. I had in the meantime written some further thoughts about of the rules I had posted. People had responded positively toward those new ideas, as well. It seemed to me, therefore, that there might be a nice fit between the Quora list and my new agent's ideas. So, I sent her the list. She liked it.

At about the same time, a friend and former student of mine—the novelist and screenwriter Gregg Hurwitz—was considering a new book, which would become the bestselling thriller *Orphan X*. He liked the rules, too. He had Mia, the book's female lead, post a selection of them, one by one, on her fridge, at points in the story where they seemed apropos. That was another piece of evidence supporting my supposition of their attractiveness. I suggested to my agent that I write a brief chapter on each of the rules. She agreed, so I wrote a book proposal suggesting as much. When I started writing the actual chapters, however, they weren't at all brief. I had much more to say about each rule than I originally envisioned.

This was partly because I had spent a very long time researching my first book: studying history, mythology, neuroscience, psychoanalysis, child psychology, poetry, and large sections of the Bible. I read and perhaps even understood much of Milton's *Paradise Lost,* Goethe's *Faust* and Dante's *Inferno.* I integrated all of that, for better or worse, trying to address a perplexing problem: the reason or reasons for the nuclear standoff of the Cold War. I couldn't understand how belief systems could be so important to people that they were willing to risk the destruction of the world to protect them. I came to realize that shared belief systems made people intelligible to one another—and that the systems weren't just about belief.

People who live by the same code are rendered mutually predictable to one another. They act in keeping with each other's expectations and desires. They can cooperate. They can even compete peacefully, because everyone knows what to expect from everyone else. A shared belief system, partly psychological, partly acted out, simplifies everyone—in their own eyes, and in the eyes of others. Shared beliefs simplify the world, as well, because people who know what to expect from one another can act together to tame the world. There is perhaps nothing more important than the maintenance of this organization—this simplification. If it's threatened, the great ship of state rocks.

It isn't precisely that people will fight for what they believe. They will fight, instead, to maintain *the match between* what they believe, what they expect, and what they desire. They will fight to maintain the match between what they expect and how everyone is acting. It is precisely the maintenance of that match that enables everyone to live together peacefully, predictably and productively. It reduces uncertainty and the chaotic mix of intolerable emotions that uncertainty inevitably produces.

Imagine someone betrayed by a trusted lover. The sacred social contract obtaining between the two has been violated. Actions speak louder than words, and an act of betrayal disrupts the fragile and carefully negotiated peace of an intimate relationship. In the aftermath of disloyalty, people are seized by terrible emotions: disgust, contempt (for self and traitor), guilt, anxiety, rage and dread. Conflict is inevitable, sometimes with deadly results. Shared belief systems—shared systems of agreed-upon conduct and expectation—regulate and control all those powerful forces. It's no wonder that people will fight to protect something that saves them from being possessed by emotions of chaos and terror (and after that from degeneration into strife and combat).

There's more to it, too. A shared cultural system stabilizes human interaction, but is also a system of value—a hierarchy of value, where some things are given priority and importance and others are not. In the absence of such a system of value, people simply cannot act. In fact, they can't even perceive, because both action and perception require a goal, and a valid goal is, by necessity, something valued. We experience much of our positive emotion in relation to goals. We are not happy, technically speaking, unless we see ourselves progressing—and the very idea of progression implies value. Worse yet is the fact that the meaning of life without positive value is not simply neutral. Because we are vulnerable and mortal, pain and anxiety are an integral part of human existence. We must have something to set against the suffering that is intrinsic to Being. [fn2] We must have the meaning inherent in a profound system of value or the horror of existence rapidly becomes paramount. Then, nihilism beckons, with its hopelessness and despair.

So: no value, no meaning. Between value systems, however, there is the possibility of conflict. We are thus eternally caught between the most diamantine rock and the hardest of places: loss of group-centred belief renders life chaotic, miserable, intolerable; presence of group-centred belief makes conflict with other groups inevitable. In the West, we have been withdrawing from our tradition-, religion- and even nation-centred cultures, partly to decrease the danger of group conflict. But we are increasingly falling prey to the desperation of meaninglessness, and that is no improvement at all.

While writing *Maps of Meaning*, I was (also) driven by the realization that we can no longer afford conflict—certainly not on the scale of the world conflagrations of the twentieth century. Our technologies of destruction have become too powerful. The potential consequences of war are literally apocalyptic. But we cannot simply abandon our systems of value, our beliefs, our cultures, either. I agonized over this apparently intractable problem for months. Was there a third way, invisible to me? I dreamt one night during this period that I was suspended in mid-air, clinging to a chandelier, many stories above the ground, directly under the dome of a massive cathedral. The people on the floor below were distant and tiny. There was a great expanse between me and any wall—and even the peak of the dome itself.

I have learned to pay attention to dreams, not least because of my training as a clinical psychologist. Dreams shed light on the dim places where reason itself has yet to voyage. I have studied Christianity a fair bit, too (more than other religious traditions, although I am always trying to redress this lack). Like others, therefore, I must and do draw more from what I do know than from what I do not. I knew that cathedrals were constructed in the shape of a cross, and that the point under the dome was the centre of the cross. I knew that the cross was simultaneously, the point of greatest suffering, the point of death and transformation, and the symbolic centre of the world. That was not somewhere I wanted to be. I managed to get down, out of the heights—out of the symbolic sky—back to safe, familiar, anonymous ground. I don't know how. Then, still in my dream, I returned to my bedroom and my bed and tried to return to sleep and the peace of unconsciousness. As I relaxed, however, I could feel my body transported. A great wind was dissolving me, preparing to propel me back to the cathedral, to place me once again at that central point. There was no escape. It was a true nightmare. I forced myself awake. The curtains behind me were blowing in over my pillows. Half asleep, I looked at the foot of the bed. I saw the great cathedral doors. I shook myself completely awake and they disappeared.

My dream placed me at the centre of Being itself, and there was no escape. It took me months to understand what this meant. During this time, I came to a more complete, personal realization of what the great stories of the past continually insist upon: the centre is occupied by the individual. The centre is marked by the cross, as X marks the spot. Existence at that cross is suffering and transformation—and that fact, above all, needs to be voluntarily accepted. It is possible to transcend slavish adherence to the group and its doctrines and, simultaneously, to avoid the pitfalls of its opposite extreme, nihilism. It is possible, instead, to find sufficient meaning in individual consciousness and experience.

How could the world be freed from the terrible dilemma of conflict, on the one hand, and psychological and social dissolution, on the other? The answer was this: through the elevation and development of the individual, and through the willingness of everyone to shoulder the burden of Being and to take the heroic path. We must each adopt as much responsibility as possible for individual life, society and the world. We must each tell the truth and repair what is in disrepair and break down and recreate what is old and outdated. It is in this manner that we can and must reduce the suffering that poisons the world. It's asking a lot. It's asking for everything. But the alternative—the horror of authoritarian belief, the chaos of the collapsed state, the tragic catastrophe of the unbridled natural world, the existential angst and weakness of the purposeless individual—is clearly worse.

I have been thinking and lecturing about such ideas for decades. I have built up a large corpus of stories and concepts pertaining to them. I am not for a moment claiming, however, that I am entirely correct or complete in my thinking. Being is far more complicated than one person can know, and I don't have the whole story. I'm simply offering the best I can manage.

In any case, the consequence of all that previous research and thinking was the new essays which eventually became this book. My initial idea was to write a short essay on all forty of the answers I had provided to Quora. That proposal was accepted by Penguin Random House Canada. While writing, however, I cut the essay number to twenty-five and then to sixteen and then finally, to the current twelve. I've been editing that remainder, with the help and care of my official editor (and with the vicious and horribly accurate criticism of Hurwitz, mentioned previously) for the past three years.

It took a long time to settle on a title: *12 Rules for Life: An Antidote to Chaos.* Why did that one rise up above all others? First and foremost, because of its simplicity. It indicates clearly that people need ordering principles, and that chaos otherwise beckons. We require rules, standards, values—alone and together. We're pack animals, beasts of burden. We must bear a load, to justify our miserable existence. We require routine and tradition. That's order. Order can become excessive, and that's not good, but chaos can swamp us, so we drown—and that is also not good. We need to stay on the straight and narrow path. Each of the twelve rules of this book—and their accompanying essays—therefore provide a guide to being there. "There" is the dividing line between order and chaos. That's where we are simultaneously stable enough, exploring enough, transforming enough, repairing enough, and cooperating enough. It's there we find the meaning that justifies life and its inevitable suffering. Perhaps, if we lived properly, we would be able to tolerate the weight of our own self-consciousness. Perhaps, if we lived properly, we could withstand the knowledge of our own fragility and mortality, without the sense of aggrieved victimhood that produces, first, resentment, then envy, and then the desire for vengeance and destruction. Perhaps, if we lived properly, we wouldn't have to turn to totalitarian certainty to shield ourselves from the knowledge of our own insufficiency and ignorance. Perhaps we could come to avoid those pathways to Hell—and we have seen in the terrible twentieth century just how real Hell can be.

I hope that these rules and their accompanying essays will help people understand what they already know: that the soul of the individual eternally hungers for the heroism of genuine Being, and that the willingness to take on that responsibility is identical to the decision to live a meaningful life.

If we each live properly, we will collectively flourish.

Best wishes to you all, as you proceed through these pages.

Dr. Jordan B. Peterson
Clinical Psychologist and Professor of Psychology

ASSUME THAT THE PERSON YOU ARE LISTENING TO MIGHT KNOW SOMETHING YOU DON'T

NOT ADVICE

Psychotherapy is not advice. Advice is what you get when the person you're talking with about something horrible and complicated wishes you would just shut up and go away. Advice is what you get when the person you are talking to wants to revel in the superiority of his or her own intelligence. If you weren't so stupid, after all, you wouldn't have your stupid problems.

Psychotherapy is genuine conversation. Genuine conversation is exploration, articulation and strategizing. When you're involved in a genuine conversation, you're listening, and talking—but mostly listening. Listening is paying attention. It's amazing what people will tell you if you listen. Sometimes if you listen to people they will even tell you what's wrong with them. Sometimes they will even tell you how they plan to fix it. Sometimes that helps you fix something wrong with yourself. One surprising time (and this is only one occasion of many when such things happened), I was listening to someone very carefully, and she told me within minutes (a) that she was a witch and (b) that her witch coven spent a lot of its time visualizing world peace together. She was a long-time lower-level functionary in some bureaucratic job. I would never have guessed that she was a witch. I also didn't know that witch covens spent any of their time visualizing world peace. I didn't know what to make of any of it, either, but it wasn't boring, and that's something.

In my clinical practice, I talk and I listen. I talk more to some people, and listen more to others. Many of the people I listen to have no one else to talk to. Some of them are truly alone in the world. There are far more people like that than you think. You don't meet them, because they are alone. Others are surrounded by tyrants or narcissists or drunks or traumatized people or professional victims. Some are not good at articulating themselves. They go off on tangents. They repeat themselves. They say vague and contradictory things. They're hard to listen to. Others have terrible things happening around them. They have parents with Alzheimer's or sick children. There's not much time left over for their personal concerns.

One time a client who I had been seeing for a few months came into my office [fn1] for her scheduled appointment and, after some brief preliminaries, she announced "I think I was raped." It is not easy to know how to respond to a statement like that, although there is frequently some mystery around such events. Often alcohol is involved, as it is in most sexual assault cases. Alcohol can cause ambiguity. That's partly why people drink. Alcohol temporarily lifts the terrible burden of self-consciousness from people. Drunk people know about the future, but they don't care about it. That's exciting. That's exhilarating. Drunk people can party like there's no tomorrow. But, because there is a tomorrow—most of the time—drunk people also get in trouble. They black out. They go to dangerous places with careless people. They have fun. But they also get raped. So, I immediately thought something like that might be involved. How else to understand "I think"? But that wasn't the end of the story. She added an extra detail: "Five times." The first sentence was awful enough, but the second produced something unfathomable. Five times? What could that possibly mean?

My client told me that she would go to a bar and have a few drinks. Someone would start to talk with her. She would end up at his place or her place with him. The evening would proceed, inevitably, to its sexual climax. The next day she would wake up, uncertain about what happened—uncertain about her motives, uncertain about his motives, and uncertain about the world. Miss S, we'll call her, was vague to the point of non-existence. She was a ghost of a person. She dressed, however, like a professional. She knew how to present herself, for first appearances. In consequence, she had finagled her way onto a government advisory board considering the construction of a major piece of transportation infrastructure (even though she knew nothing about government, advising or construction). She also hosted a local public-access radio show dedicated to small business, even though she had never held a real job, and knew nothing about being an entrepreneur. She had been receiving welfare payments for the entirety of her adulthood.

Her parents had never provided her with a minute of attention. She had four brothers and they were not at all good to her. She had no friends now, and none in the past. She had no partner. She had no one to talk to, and she didn't know how to think on her own (that's not rare). She had no self. She was, instead, a walking cacophony of unintegrated experiences. I had tried previously to help her find a job. I asked her if she had a CV. She said yes. I asked her to bring it to me. She brought it to our next session. It was fifty pages long. It was in a file folder box, divided into sections, with manila tag separators—the ones with the little colorful index-markers on the sides. The sections included such topics as "My Dreams" and "Books I Have Read." She had written down dozens of her night-time dreams in the "My Dreams" section, and provided brief summaries and reviews of her reading material. This was what she proposed to send to prospective employers (or perhaps already had: who really knew?). It is impossible to understand how much someone has to be no one at all to exist in a world where a file folder box containing fifty indexed pages listing dreams and novels constitutes a CV. Miss S knew nothing about herself. She knew nothing about other individuals. She knew nothing about the world. She was a movie played out of focus. And she was desperately waiting for a story about herself to make it all make sense.

If you add some sugar to cold water, and stir it, the sugar will dissolve. If you heat up that water, you can dissolve more. If you heat the water to boiling, you can add a lot more sugar and get that to dissolve too. Then, if you take that boiling sugar water, and slowly cool it, and don't bump it or jar it, you can trick it (I don't know how else to phrase this) into holding a lot more dissolved sugar than it would have it if it had remained cold all along. That's called a super-saturated solution. If you drop a single crystal of sugar into that super-saturated solution, all the excess sugar will suddenly and dramatically crystallize. It's as if it were crying out for order. That was my client. People like her are the reason that the many forms of psychotherapy currently practised all work. People can be so confused that their psyches will be ordered and their lives improved by the adoption of any reasonably orderly system of interpretation. This is the bringing together of the disparate elements of their lives in a disciplined manner—any disciplined manner. So, if you have come apart at the seams (or if you never have been together at all) you can restructure your life on Freudian, Jungian, Adlerian, Rogerian or behavioural principles. At least then you make sense. At least then you're coherent. At least then you might be good for something, if not good yet for everything. You can't fix a car with an axe, but you can cut down a tree. That's still something.

At about the same time I was seeing this client, the media was all afire with stories of recovered memories—particularly of sexual assault. The dispute raged apace: were these genuine accounts of past trauma? Or were they post-hoc constructs, dreamed up as a consequence of pressure wittingly or unwittingly applied by incautious therapists, grasped onto desperately by clinical clients all-too-eager to find a simple cause for all their trouble? Sometimes, it was the former, perhaps; and sometimes the latter. I understood much more clearly and precisely, however, how easy it might be to instill a false memory into the mental landscape as soon as my client revealed her uncertainty about her sexual experiences. The past appears fixed, but it's not —not in an important psychological sense. There is an awful lot to the past, after all, and the way we organize it can be subject to drastic revision.

Imagine, for example, a movie where nothing but terrible things happen. But, in the end, everything works out. Everything is resolved. A sufficiently happy ending can change the meaning of all the previous events. They can all be viewed as worthwhile, given that ending. Now imagine another movie. A lot of things are happening. They're all exciting and interesting. But there are a lot of them. Ninety minutes in, you start to worry. "This is a great movie," you think, "but there are a lot of things going on. I sure hope the filmmaker can pull it all together." But that doesn't happen. Instead, the story ends, abruptly, unresolved, or something facile and clichéd occurs. You leave deeply annoyed and unsatisfied—failing to notice that you were fully engaged and enjoying the movie almost the whole time you were in the theatre. The present can change the past, and the future can change the present.

When you are remembering the past, as well, you remember some parts of it and forget others. You have clear memories of some things that happened, but not others, of potentially equal import—just as in the present you are aware of some aspects of your surroundings and unconscious of others. You categorize your experience, grouping some elements together, and separating them from the rest. There is a mysterious arbitrariness about all of this. You don't form a comprehensive, objective record. You can't. You just don't know enough. You just can't perceive enough. You're not objective, either. You're alive. You're subjective. You have vested interests—at least in yourself, at least usually. What exactly should be included in the story? Where exactly is the border between events?

The sexual abuse of children is distressingly common.[156] However, it's not as common as poorly trained psychotherapists think, and it also does not always produce terribly damaged adults.[157] People vary in their resilience. An event that will wipe one person out can be shrugged off by another. But therapists with a little second-hand knowledge of Freud often axiomatically assume that a distressed adult in their practice must have been subject to childhood sexual abuse. Why else would they be distressed? So, they dig, and infer, and intimate, and suggest, and overreact, and bias and tilt. They exaggerate the importance of some events, and downplay the importance of others. They trim the facts to fit their theory.[158] And they convince their clients that they were sexually abused—if they could only remember. And then the clients start to remember. And then they start to accuse. And sometimes what they remember never happened, and the people accused are innocent. The good news? At least the therapist's theory remains intact. That's good—for the therapist. But there's no shortage of collateral damage. However, people are often willing to produce a lot of collateral damage if they can retain their theory.

I knew about all this when Miss S came to talk to me about her sexual experiences. When she recounted her trips to the singles bars, and their recurring aftermath, I thought a bunch of things at once. I thought, "You're so vague and so non-existent. You're a denizen of chaos and the underworld. You are going ten different places at the same time. Anyone can take you by the hand and guide you down the road of their choosing." After all, if you're not the leading man in your own drama, you're a bit player in someone else's —and you might well be assigned to play a dismal, lonely and tragic part. After Miss S recounted her story, we sat there. I thought, "You have normal sexual desires. You're extremely lonely. You're unfulfilled sexually. You're afraid of men and ignorant of the world and know nothing of yourself. You

wander around like an accident waiting to happen and the accident happens
and that's your life."

I thought, "Part of you wants to be taken. Part of you wants to be a child.
You were abused by your brothers and ignored by your father and so part of
you wants revenge upon men. Part of you is guilty. Another part is ashamed.
Another part is thrilled and excited. Who are you? What did you do? What
happened?" What was the objective truth? There was no way of knowing the
objective truth. And there never would be. There was no objective observer,
and there never would be. There was no complete and accurate story. Such a
thing did not and could not exist. There were, and are, only partial accounts
and fragmentary viewpoints. But some are still better than others. Memory is
not a description of the objective past. *Memory is a tool*. Memory is the
past's guide to the future. If you remember that something bad happened, and
you can figure out why, then you can try to avoid that bad thing happening
again. That's the purpose of memory. It's not "to remember the past." It's to
stop the same damn thing from happening over and over.

I thought, "I could simplify Miss S's life. I could say that her suspicions of
rape were fully justified, and that her doubt about the events was nothing but
additional evidence of her thorough and long-term victimization. I could
insist that her sexual partners had a legal obligation to ensure that she was not
too impaired by alcohol to give consent. I could tell her that she had
indisputably been subject to violent and illicit acts, unless she had consented
to each sexual move explicitly and verbally. I could tell her that she was an
innocent victim." I could have told her all that. And it would have been true.
And she would have accepted it as true, and remembered it for the rest of her
life. She would have been a new person, with a new history, and a new
destiny.

But I also thought, "I could tell Miss S that she is a walking disaster. I
could tell her that she wanders into a bar like a courtesan in a coma, that she
is a danger to herself and others, that she needs to wake up, and that if she
goes to singles bars and drinks too much and is taken home and has rough
violent sex (or even tender caring sex), then what the hell does she expect?"
In other words, I could have told her, in more philosophical terms, that she
was Nietzsche's "pale criminal"—the person who at one moment dares to
break the sacred law and at the next shrinks from paying the price. And that

would have been true, too, and she would have accepted it as such, and remembered it.

If I had been the adherent of a left-wing, social-justice ideology, I would have told her the first story. If I had been the adherent of a conservative ideology, I would have told her the second. And her responses after having been told either the first or the second story would have proved to my satisfaction and hers that the story I had told her was true—completely, irrefutably true. And that would have been advice.

Figure It Out for Yourself

I decided instead to listen. I have learned not to steal my clients' problems from them. I don't want to be the redeeming hero or the *deus ex machina*—not in someone else's story. I don't want their lives. So, I asked her to tell me what she thought, and I listened. She talked a lot. When we were finished, she still didn't know if she had been raped, and neither did I. Life is very complicated.

Sometimes you have to change the way you understand everything to properly understand a single something. "Was I raped?" can be a very complicated question. The mere fact that the question would present itself in that form indicates the existence of infinite layers of complexity—to say nothing of "five times." There are a myriad of questions hidden inside "Was I raped?": What is rape? What is consent? What constitutes appropriate sexual caution? How should a person defend herself? Where does the fault lie? "Was I raped?" is a hydra. If you cut off the head of a hydra, seven more grow. That's life. Miss S would have had to talk for twenty years to figure out whether she had been raped. And someone would have had to be there to listen. I started the process, but circumstances made it impossible for me to finish. She left therapy with me only somewhat less ill-formed and vague than when she first met me. But at least she didn't leave as the living embodiment of my damned ideology.

The people I listen to need to talk, because that's how people think. People need to think. Otherwise they wander blindly into pits. When people think, they simulate the world, and plan how to act in it. If they do a good job of simulating, they can figure out what stupid things they shouldn't do. Then they can not do them. Then they don't have to suffer the consequences.

That's the purpose of thinking. But we can't do it alone. We simulate the world, and plan our actions in it. Only human beings do this. That's how brilliant we are. We make little avatars of ourselves. We place those avatars in fictional worlds. Then we watch what happens. If our avatar thrives, then we act like he does, in the real world. Then we thrive (we hope). If our avatar fails, we don't go there, if we have any sense. We let him die in the fictional world, so that we don't have to really die in the present.

Imagine two children talking. The younger one says, "Wouldn't it be fun to climb up on the roof?" He has just placed a little avatar of himself in a fictional world. But his older sister objects. She chimes in. "That's stupid," she says. "What if you fall off the roof? What if Dad catches you?" The younger child can then modify the original simulation, draw the appropriate conclusion, and let the whole fictional world wither on the vine. Or not. Maybe the risk is worth it. But at least now it can be factored in. The fictional world is a bit more complete, and the avatar a bit wiser.

People think they think, but it's not true. It's mostly self-criticism that passes for thinking. True thinking is rare—just like true listening. Thinking is listening to yourself. It's difficult. To think, you have to be at least two people at the same time. Then you have to let those people disagree. Thinking is an internal dialogue between two or more different views of the world. Viewpoint One is an avatar in a simulated world. It has its own representations of past, present and future, and its own ideas about how to act. So do Viewpoints Two, and Three, and Four. Thinking is the process by which these internal avatars imagine and articulate their worlds to one another. You can't set straw men against one another when you're thinking, either, because then you're not thinking. You're rationalizing, post-hoc. You're matching what you want against a weak opponent so that you don't have to change your mind. You're propagandizing. You're using double-speak. You're using your conclusions to justify your proofs. You're hiding from the truth.

True thinking is complex and demanding. It requires you to be articulate speaker and careful, judicious listener, at the same time. It involves conflict. So, you have to tolerate conflict. Conflict involves negotiation and compromise. So, you have to learn to give and take and to modify your premises and adjust your thoughts—even your perceptions of the world. Sometimes it results in the defeat and elimination of one or more internal avatar. They don't like to be defeated or eliminated, either. They're hard to build. They're valuable. They're alive. They like to stay alive. They'll fight to stay alive. You better listen to them. If you don't they'll go underground and turn into devils and torture you. In consequence, thinking is emotionally painful, as well as physiologically demanding; more so than anything else— except not thinking. But you have to be very articulate and sophisticated to have all of this occur inside your own head. What are you to do, then, if you aren't very good at thinking, at being two people at one time? That's easy. You talk. But you need someone to listen. A listening person is your collaborator and your opponent.

A listening person tests your talking (and your thinking) without having to say anything. A listening person is a representative of common humanity. He stands for the crowd. Now the crowd is by no means always right, but it's *commonly* right. It's *typically* right. If you say something that takes everyone aback, therefore, you should reconsider what you said. I say that, knowing full well that controversial opinions are sometimes correct—sometimes so much so that the crowd will perish if it refuses to listen. It is for this reason, among others, that the individual is morally obliged to stand up and tell the truth of his or her own experience. But something new and radical is still almost always wrong. You need good, even great, reasons to ignore or defy general, public opinion. That's your culture. It's a mighty oak. You perch on one of its branches. If the branch breaks, it's a long way down—farther, perhaps, than you think. If you're reading this book, there's a strong probability that you're a privileged person. You can read. You have time to read. You're perched high in the clouds. It took untold generations to get you where you are. A little gratitude might be in order. If you're going to insist on bending the world to your way, you better have your reasons. If you're going to stand your ground, you better have your reasons. You better have thought them through. You might otherwise be in for a very hard landing. You should do what other people do, unless you have a very good reason not to. If you're in a rut, at least you know that other people have travelled that path. Out of the rut is too often off the road. And in the desert that awaits off the road there are highwaymen and monsters.

So speaks wisdom.

A Listening Person

A listening person can reflect the crowd. He can do that without talking. He can do that merely by letting the talking person listen to himself. That is what Freud recommended. He had his patients lay on a couch, look at the ceiling, let their minds wander, and say whatever wandered in. That's his method of *free association.* That's the way the Freudian psychoanalyst avoids transferring his or her own personal biases and opinions into the internal landscape of the patient. It was for such reasons that Freud did not face his patients. He did not want their spontaneous meditations to be altered by his emotional expressions, no matter how slight. He was properly concerned that his own opinions—and, worse, his own unresolved problems—would find themselves uncontrollably reflected in his responses and reactions, conscious and unconscious alike. He was afraid that he would in such a manner detrimentally affect the development of his patients. It was for such reasons, as well, that Freud insisted that psychoanalysts be analyzed themselves. He wanted those who practiced his method to uncover and eliminate some of their own worst blind spots and prejudices, so they would not practise corruptly. Freud had a point. He was, after all, a genius. You can tell that because people still hate him. But there are disadvantages to the detached and somewhat distant approach recommended by Freud. Many of those who seek therapy desire and need a closer, more personal relationship (although that also has its dangers). This is in part why I have opted in my practice for the conversation, instead of the Freudian method—as have most clinical psychologists.

It can be worthwhile for my clients to see my reactions. To protect them from the undue influence that might produce, I attempt to set my aim properly, so that my responses emerge from the appropriate motivation. I do what I can to want the best for them (whatever that might be). I do my best to want the best, period, as well (because that is part of wanting the best for my clients). I try to clear my mind, and to leave my own concerns aside. That way I am concentrating on what is best for my clients, while I am simultaneously alert to any cues that I might be misunderstanding what that best is. That's something that has to be negotiated, not assumed on my part. It's something that has to be managed very carefully, to mitigate the risks of close, personal interaction. My clients talk. I listen. Sometimes I respond.

Often the response is subtle. It's not even verbal. My clients and I face each other. We make eye contact. We can see each other's expressions. They can observe the effects of their words on me, and I can observe the effects of mine on them. They can respond to my responses.

A client of mine might say, "I hate my wife." It's out there, once said. It's hanging in the air. It has emerged from the underworld, materialized from chaos, and manifested itself. It is perceptible and concrete and no longer easily ignored. It's become real. The speaker has even startled himself. He sees the same thing reflected in my eyes. He notes that, and continues on the road to sanity. "Hold it," he says. "Back up. That's too harsh. *Sometimes* I hate my wife. I hate her when she won't tell me what she wants. My mom did that all the time, too. It drove Dad crazy. It drove all of us crazy, to tell you the truth. It even drove Mom crazy! She was a nice person, but she was very resentful. Well, at least my wife isn't as bad as my mother. Not at all. Wait! I guess my wife is actually pretty good at telling me what she wants, but I get really bothered when she doesn't, because Mom tortured us all half to death being a martyr. That really affected me. Maybe I overreact now when it happens even a bit. Hey! I'm acting just like Dad did when Mom upset him! That isn't me. That doesn't have anything to do with my wife! I better let her know." I observe from all this that my client had failed previously to properly distinguish his wife from his mother. And I see that he was possessed, unconsciously, by the spirit of his father. He sees all of that too. Now he is a bit more differentiated, a bit less an uncarved block, a bit less hidden in the fog. He has sewed up a small tear in the fabric of his culture. He says, "That was a good session, Dr. Peterson." I nod. You can be pretty smart if you can just shut up.

I'm a collaborator and opponent even when I'm not talking. I can't help it. My expressions broadcast my response, even when they're subtle. So, I'm communicating, as Freud so rightly stressed, even when silent. But I also talk in my clinical sessions. How do I know when to say something? First, as I said, I put myself in the proper frame of mind. I aim properly. I want things to be better. My mind orients itself, given this goal. It tries to produce responses to the therapeutic dialogue that furthers that aim. I watch what happens, internally. I reveal my responses. That's the first rule. Sometimes, for example, a client will say something, and a thought will occur to me, or a fantasy flit through my mind. Frequently it's about something that was said by the same client earlier that day, or during a previous session. Then I tell my client that thought or fantasy. Disinterestedly. I say, "You said this and I noticed that I then became aware of this." Then we discuss it. We try to determine the relevance of meaning of my reaction. Sometimes, perhaps, it's about me. That was Freud's point. But sometimes it is just the reaction of a detached but positively inclined human being to a personally revealing statement by another human being. It's meaningful—sometimes, even, corrective. Sometimes, however, it's me that gets corrected.

You have to get along with other people. A therapist is one of those other people. A good therapist will tell you the truth about what he thinks. (That is not the same thing as telling you that what he thinks is the truth.) Then at least you have the honest opinion of at least one person. That's not so easy to get. That's not nothing. That's key to the psychotherapeutic process: two people tell each other the truth—and both listen.

How Should You Listen?

Carl Rogers, one of the twentieth century's great psychotherapists, knew something about listening. He wrote, "The great majority of us cannot listen; we find ourselves compelled to evaluate, because listening is too dangerous. The first requirement is courage, and we do not always have it."[159] He knew that listening could transform people. On that, Rogers commented, "Some of you may be feeling that you listen well to people, and that you have never seen such results. The chances are very great indeed that your listening has not been of the type I have described." He suggested that his readers conduct a short experiment when they next found themselves in a dispute: "Stop the discussion for a moment, and institute this rule: 'Each person can speak up for himself only after he has first restated the ideas and feelings of the previous speaker accurately, and to that speaker's satisfaction.' " I have found this technique very useful, in my private life and in my practice. I routinely summarize what people have said to me, and ask them if I have understood properly. Sometimes they accept my summary. Sometimes I am offered a small correction. Now and then I am wrong completely. All of that is good to know.

There are several primary advantages to this process of summary. The first advantage is that I genuinely come to understand what the person is saying.

Of this, Rogers notes, "Sounds simple, doesn't it? But if you try it you will discover it is one of the most difficult things you have ever tried to do. If you really understand a person in this way, if you are willing to enter his private world and see the way life appears to him, you run the risk of being changed yourself. You might see it his way, you might find yourself influenced in your attitudes or personality. This risk of being changed is one of the most frightening prospects most of us can face." More salutary words have rarely been written.

The second advantage to the act of summary is that it aids the person in consolidation and utility of memory. Consider the following situation: A client in my practice recounts a long, meandering, emotion-laden account of a difficult period in his or her life. We summarize, back and forth. The account becomes shorter. It is now summed up, in the client's memory (and in mine) in the form we discussed. It is now a different memory, in many ways—with luck, a *better* memory. It is now less weighty. It has been distilled; reduced to the gist. We have extracted the moral of the story. It becomes a description of the cause and the result of what happened, formulated such that repetition of the tragedy and pain becomes less likely in the future. "*This* is what happened. *This* is why. *This* is what I have to do to avoid such things from now on": That's a successful memory. That's the purpose of memory. You remember the past not so that it is "accurately recorded," to say it again, but so that you are prepared for the future.

The third advantage to employing the Rogerian method is the difficulty it poses to the careless construction of straw-man arguments. When someone opposes you, it is very tempting to oversimplify, parody, or distort his or her position. This is a counterproductive game, designed both to harm the dissenter and to unjustly raise your personal status. By contrast, if you are called upon to summarize someone's position, so that the speaking person agrees with that summary, you may have to state the argument even more clearly and succinctly than the speaker has even yet managed. If you first give the devil his due, looking at his arguments from his perspective, you can (1) find the value in them, and learn something in the process, or (2) hone your positions against them (if you still believe they are wrong) and strengthen your arguments further against challenge. This will make you much stronger. Then you will no longer have to misrepresent your opponent's position (and may well have bridged at least part of the gap between the two of you). You will also be much better at withstanding your own doubts.

Sometimes it takes a long time to figure out what someone genuinely means when they are talking. This is because often they are articulating their ideas for the first time. They can't do it without wandering down blind alleys or making contradictory or even nonsensical claims. This is partly because talking (and thinking) is often more about forgetting than about remembering. To discuss an event, particularly something emotional, like a death or serious illness, is to slowly choose what to leave behind. To begin, however, much that is not necessary must be put into words. The emotion-laden speaker must recount the whole experience, in detail. Only then can the central narrative, cause and consequence, come into focus or consolidate itself. Only then can the moral of the story be derived.

Imagine that someone holds a stack of hundred-dollar bills, some of which are counterfeit. All the bills might have to be spread on a table, so that each can be seen, and any differences noted, before the genuine can be distinguished from the false. This is the sort of methodical approach you have to take when really listening to someone trying to solve a problem or communicate something important. If upon learning that some of the bills are counterfeit you too casually dismiss all of them (as you would if you were in a hurry, or otherwise unwilling to put in the effort), the person will never learn to separate wheat from chaff.

If you listen, instead, without premature judgment, people will generally tell you everything they are thinking—and with very little deceit. People will tell you the most amazing, absurd, interesting things. Very few of your conversations will be boring. (You can in fact tell whether or not you are actually listening in this manner. If the conversation is boring, you probably aren't.)

Primate Dominance–Hierarchy Manoeuvres—and Wit

Not all talking is thinking. Nor does all listening foster transformation. There are other motives for both, some of which produce much less valuable, counterproductive and even dangerous outcomes. There is the conversation, for example, where one participant is speaking merely to establish or confirm his place in the dominance hierarchy. One person begins by telling a story about some interesting occurrence, recent or past, that involved something good, bad or surprising enough to make the listening worthwhile. The other person, now concerned with his or her potentially substandard status as less-interesting individual, immediately thinks of something better, worse, or more surprising to relate. This isn't one of those situations where two conversational participants are genuinely playing off each other, riffing on the same themes, for the mutual enjoyment of both (and everyone else). This is jockeying for position, pure and simple. You can tell when one of those conversations is occurring. They are accompanied by a feeling of embarrassment among speakers and alike, all who know that something false and exaggerated has just been said.

There is another, closely allied form of conversation, where neither speaker is listening in the least to the other. Instead, each is using the time occupied by the current speaker to conjure up what he or she will say next, which will often be something off-topic, because the person anxiously waiting to speak has not been listening. This can and will bring the whole conversational train to a shuddering halt. At this point, it is usual for those who were on board during the crash to remain silent, and look occasionally and in a somewhat embarrassed manner at each other, until everyone leaves, or someone thinks of something witty and puts Humpty Dumpty together again.

Then there is the conversation where one participant is trying to attain victory for his point of view. This is yet another variant of the dominance-hierarchy conversation. During such a conversation, which often tends toward the ideological, the speaker endeavours to (1) denigrate or ridicule the viewpoint of anyone holding a contrary position, (2) use selective evidence while doing so and, finally, (3) impress the listeners (many of whom are already occupying the same ideological space) with the validity of his assertions. The goal is to gain support for a comprehensive, unitary, oversimplified world-view. Thus, the purpose of the conversation is to make the case that *not* thinking is the correct tack. The person who is speaking in this manner believes that winning the argument makes him right, and that doing so necessarily validates the assumption-structure of the dominance hierarchy he most identifies with. This is often—and unsurprisingly—the hierarchy within which he has achieved the most success, or the one with which he is most temperamentally aligned. Almost all discussions involving politics or economics unfold in this manner, with each participant attempting to justify fixed, *a priori* positions instead of trying to learn something or to adopt a different frame (even for the novelty). It is for this reason that conservatives and liberals alike believe their positions to be self-evident, particularly as they become more extreme. Given certain temperamentally-based assumptions, a predictable conclusion emerges—but only when you ignore the fact that the assumptions themselves are mutable.

These conversations are very different from the listening type. When a genuine listening conversation is taking place, one person at a time has the floor, and everyone else is listening. The person speaking is granted the opportunity to seriously discuss some event, usually unhappy or even tragic. Everyone else responds sympathetically. These conversations are important because the speaker is organizing the troublesome event in his or her mind, while recounting the story. The fact is important enough to bear repeating: people organize their brains with conversation. If they don't have anyone to tell their story to, they lose their minds. Like hoarders, they cannot unclutter themselves. The input of the community is required for the integrity of the individual psyche. To put it another way: It takes a village to organize a mind.

Much of what we consider healthy mental function is the result of our ability to use the reactions of others to keep our complex selves functional. *We outsource the problem of our sanity.* This is why it is the fundamental responsibility of parents to render their children socially acceptable. If a person's behaviour is such that other people can tolerate him, then all he has to do is place himself in a social context. Then people will indicate—by being interested in or bored by what he says, or laughing or not laughing at his jokes, or teasing or ridiculing, or even by lifting an eyebrow—whether his actions and statements are what they should be. Everyone is always broadcasting to everyone else their desire to encounter the ideal. We punish and reward each other precisely to the degree that each of us behaves in keeping with that desire—except, of course, when we are looking for trouble.

The sympathetic responses offered during a genuine conversation indicate that the teller is valued, and that the story being told is important, serious, deserving of consideration, and understandable. Men and women often misunderstand each other when these conversations are focused on a specified problem. Men are often accused of wanting to "fix things" too early on in a discussion. This frustrates men, who like to solve problems and to do it efficiently and who are in fact called upon frequently by women for precisely that purpose. It might be easier for my male readers to understand why this does not work, however, if they could realize and then remember that before a problem can be solved it must be formulated precisely. Women are often intent on formulating the problem when they are discussing something, and they need to be listened to—even questioned—to help ensure clarity in the formulation. Then, whatever problem is left, if any, can be helpfully solved. (It should also be noted first that too-early problem-solving may also merely indicate a desire to escape from the effort of the problem-formulating conversation.)

Another conversational variant is the lecture. A lecture is—somewhat surprisingly—a conversation. The lecturer speaks, but the audience communicates with him or her non-verbally. A surprising amount of human interaction—much of the delivery of emotional information, for example—takes place in this manner, through postural display and facial emotion (as we noted in our discussion of Freud). A good lecturer is not only delivering facts (which is perhaps the least important part of a lecture), but also telling stories about those facts, pitching them precisely to the level of the audience's comprehension, gauging that by the interest they are showing. The story he or she is telling conveys to the members of the audience not only what the facts are, but *why* they are relevant—why it is important to know certain things about which they are currently ignorant. To demonstrate the importance of some set of facts is to tell those audience members how such knowledge could change their behaviour, or influence the way they interpret the world, so that they will now be able to avoid some obstacles and progress more rapidly to some better goals.

A good lecturer is thus talking *with* and not *at* or even *to* his or her listeners. To manage this, the lecturer needs to be closely attending to the audience's every move, gesture and sound. Perversely, *this cannot be done by watching the audience, as such.* A good lecturer speaks directly to and watches the response of single, identifiable people, [fn2] instead of doing something clichéd, such as "presenting a talk" to an audience. Everything about that phrase is wrong. You don't present. You talk. There is no such thing as "a talk," unless it's canned, and it shouldn't be. There is also no "audience." There are *individuals,* who need to be included in the conversation. A well-practised and competent public speaker addresses a single, identifiable person, watches that individual nod, shake his head, frown, or look confused, and responds appropriately and directly to those gestures and expressions. Then, after a few phrases, rounding out some idea, he switches to another audience member, and does the same thing. In this manner, he infers and reacts to the attitude of the entire group (insofar as such a thing exists).

There are still other conversations that work primarily as demonstrations of wit. These also have a dominance element, but the goal is to be the most entertaining speaker (which is an accomplishment that everyone participating will also enjoy). The purpose of these conversations, as a witty friend of mine once observed, was to say "anything that was either true or funny." As truth and humour are often close allies, that combination worked fine. I think that this might be the intelligent blue-collar worker's conversation. I participated in many fine bouts of sarcasm, satire, insult and generally over-the-top comedic exchange around among people I grew up with in Northern Alberta and, later, among some Navy SEALs I met in California, who were friends of an author I know who writes somewhat horrifying popular fiction. They were all perfectly happy to say anything, no matter how appalling, as long it was funny.

I attended this writer's fortieth birthday celebration not too long ago in LA. He had invited one of the aforementioned SEALs. A few months beforehand, however, his wife had been diagnosed with a serious medical condition, necessitating brain surgery. He called up his SEAL friend, informed him of the circumstances, and indicated that the event might have to be cancelled. "You think you guys have a problem," responded his friend. "I just bought non-refundable airline tickets to your party!" It's not clear what percentage of the world's population would find that response amusing. I retold the story recently to a group of newer acquaintances and they were more shocked and appalled than amused. I tried to defend the joke as an indication of the SEAL's respect for the couple's ability to withstand and transcend tragedy, but I wasn't particularly successful. Nonetheless, I believe that he did intend exactly that respect, and I think he was terrifyingly witty. His joke was daring, anarchic to the point of recklessness, which is exactly the point where serious funny occurs. My friend and his wife recognized the compliment. They saw that their friend knew they were tough enough to withstand that level of—well, let's call it competitive humour. It was a test of character, which they passed with flying colours.

I found that such conversations occurred less and less frequently as I moved from university to university, up the educational and social ladder. Maybe it wasn't a class thing, although I have my suspicions it was. Maybe it's just that I'm older, or that the friends a person makes later in life, after adolescence, lack the insane competitive closeness and perverse playfulness of those early tribal bonds. When I went back up north to my hometown for my fiftieth birthday party, however, my old friends made me laugh so hard I had to duck into a different room several times to catch my breath. Those conversations are the most fun, and I miss them. You have to keep up, or risk severe humiliation, but there is nothing more rewarding than topping the last comedian's story, joke, insult or curse. Only one rule really applies: do not be boring (although it is also very bad form to *actually* put someone down, when you are only *pretending* to put them down).

Conversation on the Way

The final type of conversation, akin to listening, is a form of mutual exploration. It requires true reciprocity on the part of those listening and speaking. It allows all participants to express and organize their thoughts. A conversation of mutual exploration has a topic, generally complex, of genuine interest to the participants. Everyone participating is trying to solve a problem, instead of insisting on the *a priori* validity of their own positions. All are acting on the premise that they have something to learn. This kind of conversation constitutes active philosophy, the highest form of thought, and the best preparation for proper living.

The people involved in such a conversation must be discussing ideas they genuinely use to structure their perceptions and guide their actions and words. They must be existentially involved with their philosophy: that is, they must be living it, not merely believing or understanding it. They also must have inverted, at least temporarily, the typical human preference for order over chaos (and I don't mean the chaos typical of mindless antisocial rebellion). Other conversational types—except for the listening type—all attempt to buttress some existing order. The conversation of mutual exploration, by contrast, requires people who have decided that the unknown makes a better friend than the known.

You already know what you know, after all—and, unless your life is perfect, what you know is not enough. You remain threatened by disease, and self-deception, and unhappiness, and malevolence, and betrayal, and corruption, and pain, and limitation. You are subject to all these things, in the final analysis, because you are just too ignorant to protect yourself. If you just knew enough, you could be healthier and more honest. You would suffer less. You could recognize, resist and even triumph over malevolence and evil. You would neither betray a friend, nor deal falsely and deceitfully in business, politics or love. However, your current knowledge has neither made you perfect nor kept you safe. So, it is insufficient, by definition—radically, fatally insufficient.

You must accept this before you can converse philosophically, instead of convincing, oppressing, dominating or even amusing. You must accept this before you can tolerate a conversation where the Word that eternally mediates between order and chaos is operating, psychologically speaking. To have this kind of conversation, it is necessary to respect the personal experience of your conversational partners. You must assume that they have reached careful, thoughtful, genuine conclusions (and, perhaps, they must have done the work that justifies this assumption). You must believe that if they shared their conclusions with you, you could bypass at least some of the pain of personally learning the same things (as learning from the experience of others can be quicker and much less dangerous). You must meditate, too, instead of strategizing towards victory. If you fail, or refuse, to do so, then you merely and automatically repeat what you already believe, seeking its validation and insisting on its rightness. But if you are meditating as you converse, then you listen to the other person, and say the new and original things that can rise from deep within of their own accord.

It's as if you are listening to yourself during such a conversation, just as you are listening to the other person. You are describing how you are responding to the new information imparted by the speaker. You are reporting what that information has done to you—what new things it made appear within you, how it has changed your presuppositions, how it has made you think of new questions. You tell the speaker these things, directly. Then they have the same effect on him. In this manner, you both move towards somewhere newer and broader and better. You both change, as you let your old presuppositions die—as you shed your skins and emerge renewed.

A conversation such as this is one where it is the desire for truth itself—on the part of both participants—that is truly listening and speaking. That's why it's engaging, vital, interesting and meaningful. That sense of meaning is a signal from the deep, ancient parts of your Being. You're where you should be, with one foot in order, and the other tentatively extended into chaos and the unknown. You're immersed in the Tao, following the great Way of Life. There, you're stable enough to be secure, but flexible enough to transform. There, you're allowing new information to *inform* you—to permeate your stability, to repair and improve its structure, and expand its domain. There the constituent elements of your Being can find their more elegant formation. A conversation like that places you in the same place that listening to great music places you, and for much the same reason. A conversation like that puts you in the realm where souls connect, and that's a real place. It leaves you thinking, "That was really worthwhile. We really got to know each other." The masks came off, and the searchers were revealed.

So, listen, to yourself and to those with whom you are speaking. Your wisdom then consists not of the knowledge you already have, but the continual search for knowledge, which is the highest form of wisdom. It is for this reason that the priestess of the Delphic Oracle in ancient Greece spoke most highly of Socrates, who always sought the truth. She described him as the wisest living man, because he knew that what he knew was nothing.

Assume that the person you are listening to might know something you don't.

RULE 10

BE PRECISE IN YOUR SPEECH

WHY IS MY LAPTOP OBSOLETE?

What do you see, when you look at a computer—at your own laptop, more precisely? You see a flat, thin, grey-and-black box. Less evidently, you see something to type on and look at. Nonetheless, even with the second perceptions included, what are you seeing is hardly the computer at all. That grey and black box happens to be a computer right now, right here and now, and maybe even an expensive computer. Nevertheless, it will soon be something so unlike a computer that it will be difficult even to give away.

We will all discard our laptops within the next five years, even though they may still work perfectly—even though the screens, keyboards, mice and internet connections may still flawlessly perform their tasks. Fifty years from now, early twenty-first-century laptops will be oddities like the brass scientific tools of the late nineteenth century. The latter now appear more like the arcane accoutrements of alchemy, designed to measure phenomena whose existence we no longer even recognize. How can high-tech machines, each possessing more computing power than the entire Apollo space program, lose their value in such a short period of time? How can they transform so quickly from exciting, useful and status-enhancing machines to complex pieces of junk? It's because of the nature of our perceptions themselves, and the oft-invisible interaction between those perceptions and the underlying complexity of the world.

Your laptop is a note in a symphony currently being played by an orchestra of incalculable size. It's a very small part of a much greater whole. Most of its capacity resides beyond its hard shell. It maintains its function only because a vast array of other technologies are currently and harmoniously at play. It is fed, for example, by a power grid whose function is invisibly dependent on the stability of a myriad of complex physical, biological, economic and interpersonal systems. The factories that make its parts are still in operation. The operating system that enables its function is based on those parts, and not on others yet to be created. Its video hardware runs the technology expected by the creative people who post their content on the web. Your laptop is in communication with a certain, specified ecosystem of other devices and web servers.

And, finally, all this is made possible by an even less visible element: the social contract of trust—the interconnected and fundamentally honest political and economic systems that make the reliable electrical grid a reality. This interdependency of part on whole, invisible in systems that work, becomes starkly evident in systems that don't. The higher-order, surrounding systems that enable personal computing hardly exist at all in corrupt, third-world countries, so that the power lines, electrical switches, outlets, and all the other entities so hopefully and concretely indicative of such a grid are absent or compromised, and in fact make little contribution to the practical delivery of electricity to people's homes and factories. This makes perceiving the electronic and other devices that electricity theoretically enables as separate, functional units frustrating, at minimum, and impossible, at worst. This is partly because of technical insufficiency: the systems simply don't work. But it is also in no small part because of the lack of trust characteristic of systemically corrupt societies.

To put it another way: What you perceive as your computer is like a single leaf, on a tree, in a forest—or, even more accurately, like your fingers rubbing briefly across that leaf. A single leaf can be plucked from a branch. It can be perceived, briefly, as a single, self-contained entity—but that perception misleads more than clarifies. In a few weeks, the leaf will crumble and dissolve. It would not have been there at all, without the tree. It cannot continue to exist, in the absence of the tree. This is the position of our laptops in relation to the world. So much of what they are resides outside their boundaries that the screened devices we hold on our laps can only maintain their computer-like façade for a few short years.

Almost everything we see and hold is like that, although often not so evidently.

Tools, Obstacles and Extension into the World

We assume that we see objects or things when we look at the world, but that's not really how it is. Our evolved perceptual systems transform the interconnected, complex multi-level world that we inhabit not so much into *things* per se as into *useful* things (or their nemeses, things that get in the way). This is the necessary, practical reduction of the world. This is the transformation of the near-infinite complexity of things through the narrow specification of our purpose. This is how precision makes the world sensibly manifest. That is not at all the same as perceiving *objects*.

We don't see valueless entities and then attribute meaning to them. We perceive the meaning directly.[160] We see floors, to walk on, and doors, to duck through, and chairs, to sit on. It's for this reason that a beanbag and a stump both fall into the latter category, despite having little objectively in common. We see rocks, because we can throw them, and clouds, because they can rain on us, and apples, to eat, and the automobiles of other people, to get in our way and annoy us. We see tools and obstacles, not objects or things. Furthermore, we see tools and obstacles at the "handy" level of analysis that makes them most useful (or dangerous), given our needs, abilities and perceptual limitations. The world reveals itself to us as something to utilize and something to navigate through—not as something that merely is.

We see the faces of the people we are talking to, because we need to communicate with those people and cooperate with them. We don't see their microcosmic substructures, their cells, or the subcellular organelles, molecules and atoms that make up those cells. We don't see, as well, the macrocosm that surrounds them: the family members and friends that make up their immediate social circles, the economies they are embedded within, or the ecology that contains all of them. Finally, and equally importantly, we don't see them across time. We see them in the narrow, immediate, overwhelming now, instead of surrounded by the yesterdays and tomorrows that may be a more important part of them than whatever is currently and obviously manifest. And we have to see in this way, or be overwhelmed.

When we look at the world, we perceive only what is enough for our plans and actions to work and for us to get by. What we inhabit, then, is this "enough." That is a radical, functional, unconscious simplification of the world—and it's almost impossible for us not to mistake it for the world itself.

But the objects we see are not simply there, in the world, for our simple, direct perceiving. [fn1] They exist in a complex, multi-dimensional relationship to one another, not as self-evidently separate, bounded, independent objects. We perceive not them, but their functional utility and, in doing so, we make them sufficiently simple for sufficient understanding. *It is for this reason that we must be precise in our aim.* Absent that, we drown in the complexity of the world.

This is true even for our perceptions of ourselves, of our individual persons. We assume that we end at the surface of our skin, because of the way that we perceive. But we can understand with a little thought the provisional nature of that boundary. We shift what is inside our skin, so to speak, as the context we inhabit changes. Even when we do something as apparently simple as picking up a screwdriver, our brain automatically adjusts what it considers body to include the tool.[161] We can literally feel things with the end of the screwdriver. When we extend a hand, holding the screwdriver, we automatically take the length of the latter into account. We can probe nooks and crannies with its extended end, and comprehend what we are exploring. Furthermore, we instantly regard the screwdriver we are holding as "our" screwdriver, and get possessive about it. We do the same with the much more complex tools we use, in much more complex situations. The cars we pilot instantaneously and automatically become ourselves. Because of this, when someone bangs his fist on our car's hood after we have irritated him at a crosswalk, we take it personally. This is not always reasonable. Nonetheless, without the extension of self into machine, it would be impossible to drive.

The extensible boundaries of our selves also expand to include other people—family members, lovers and friends. A mother will sacrifice herself for her children. Is our father or son or wife or husband more or less integral to us than an arm or a leg? We can answer, in part, by asking: Which we rather lose? Which loss would we sacrifice more to avoid? We practice for such permanent extension—such permanent commitment—by identifying with the fictional characters of books and movies. Their tragedies and triumphs rapidly and convincingly become ours. Sitting still in our seats, we nonetheless act out a multitude of alternate realities, extending ourselves experimentally, testing multiple potential paths, before specifying the one we will actually take. Engrossed in a fictional world, we can even become things that don't "really" exist. In the blink of an eye, in the magic hall of a movie theatre, we can become fantastical creatures. We sit in the dark before rapidly flickering images and become witches, superheroes, aliens, vampires, lions, elves or wooden marionettes. We feel everything they feel, and are peculiarly happy to pay for the privilege, even when what we experience is sorrow, fear or horror.

Something similar, but more extreme, happens when we identify, not with a character in a fictional drama, but with a whole group, in a competition. Think of what happens when a favourite team wins or loses an important game against an arch-rival. The winning goal will bring the whole network of fans to their feet, before they think, in unscripted unison. It is as if their many nervous systems are directly wired to the game unfolding in front of them. Fans take the victories and defeats of their teams very personally, even wearing the jerseys of their heroes, often celebrating their wins and losses more than any such events that "actually" occur in their day-to-day lives. This identification manifests itself deeply—even biochemically and neurologically. Vicarious experiences of winning and losing, for example, raise and lower testosterone levels among fans "participating" in the contest.[162] Our capacity for identification is something that manifests itself at every level of our Being.

To the degree that we are patriotic, similarly, our country is not just *important* to us. It *is* us. We might even sacrifice our entire smaller individual selves, in battle, to maintain the integrity of our country. For much of history, such willingness to die has been regarded as something admirable and courageous, as a part of human duty. Paradoxically, that is a direct consequence not of our aggression but of our extreme sociability and willingness to cooperate. If we can become not only ourselves, but our families, teams and countries, cooperation comes easily to us, relying on the same deeply innate mechanisms that drive us (and other creatures) to protect our very bodies.

The World Is Simple Only When It Behaves

It is very difficult to make sense of the interconnected chaos of reality, just by looking at it. It's a very complicated act, requiring, perhaps, half our brains.

Everything shifts and changes in the real world. Each hypothetically separate thing is made up of smaller hypothetically separate things, and is simultaneously part of larger hypothetically separate things. The boundaries between the levels—and between different things themselves at a given level—are neither clear nor self-evident, objectively. They must be established practically, pragmatically, and they retain their validity only under very narrow and specified conditions. The conscious illusion of complete and sufficient perception only sustains itself, for example—only remains sufficient for our purposes—when everything goes according to plan. Under such circumstances, what we see is accurate enough, so that there is no utility in looking farther. To drive successfully, we don't have to understand, or even perceive, the complex machinery of our automobiles. The hidden complexities of our private cars only intrude on our consciousness when that machinery fails, or when we collide unexpectedly with something (or something with us). Even in the case of mere mechanical failure (to say nothing of a serious accident) such intrusion is always felt, at least initially, as anxiety-provoking. That's a consequence of emergent uncertainty.

A car, as we perceive it, is not a thing, or an object. It is instead something that takes us somewhere we want to go. It is only when it stops taking us and going, in fact, that we perceive it much at all. It is only when a car quits, suddenly—or is involved in an accident and must be pulled over to the side of the road—that we are forced to apprehend and analyze the myriad of parts that "car as thing that goes" depends on. When our car fails, our incompetence with regards to its complexity is instantly revealed. That has practical consequences (we don't get to go to where we were going), as well as psychological: our peace of mind disappears along with our functioning vehicle. We must generally turn to the experts who inhabit garages and workshops to restore both functionality to our vehicle and simplicity to our perceptions. That's mechanic-as-psychologist.

It is precisely then that we can understand, although we seldom deeply consider, the staggeringly low-resolution quality of our vision and the inadequacy of our corresponding understanding. In a crisis, when our thing no longer goes, we turn to those whose expertise far transcends ours to restore the match between our expectant desire and what actually happens. This all means that the failure of our car can also force us to confront the uncertainty of the broader social context, which is usually invisible to us, in which the machine (and mechanic) are mere parts. Betrayed by our car, we come up against all the things we don't know. Is it time for a new vehicle? Did I err in my original purchase? Is the mechanic competent, honest and reliable? Is the garage he works for trustworthy? Sometimes, too, we must contemplate something worse, something broader and deeper: Have the roads now become too dangerous? Have I become (or always been) too incompetent? Too scattered and inattentive? Too old? The limitations of all our perceptions of things and selves manifest themselves when something we can usually depend on in our simplified world breaks down. Then the more complex world that was always there, invisible and conveniently ignored, makes its presence known. It is then that the walled garden we archetypally inhabit reveals its hidden but ever-present snakes.

You and I Are Simple Only When the World Behaves

When things break down, what has been ignored rushes in. When things are no longer specified, with precision, the walls crumble, and chaos makes its presence known. When we've been careless, and let things slide, what we have refused to attend to gathers itself up, adopts a serpentine form, and strikes—often at the worst possible moment. It is then that we see what focused intent, precision of aim and careful attention protects us from.

Imagine a loyal and honest wife suddenly confronted by evidence of her husband's infidelity. She has lived alongside him for years. She saw him as she assumes he is: reliable, hard-working, loving, dependable. In her marriage, she is standing on a rock, or so she believes. But he becomes less attentive and more distracted. He begins, in the clichéd manner, to work longer hours. Small things she says and does irritate him unjustifiably. One day she sees him in a downtown café with another woman, interacting with her in a manner difficult to rationalize and ignore. The limitations and inaccuracy of her former perceptions become immediately and painfully obvious.

Her theory of her husband collapses. What happens, in consequence? First, something—someone—emerges in his stead: a complex, frightening stranger. That's bad enough. But it's only half the problem. Her theory of herself collapses, too, in the aftermath of the betrayal, so that it's not one stranger that's the problem: it's two. Her husband is not who she perceived him to be

—but neither is she, the betrayed wife. She is no longer the "well-loved, secure wife, and valued partner." Strangely enough, despite our belief in the permanent immutability of the past, she may never have been.

The past is not necessarily what it was, even though it has already been. The present is chaotic and indeterminate. The ground shifts continually around her feet, and ours. Equally, the future, not yet here, changes into something it was not supposed to be. Is the once reasonably content wife now a "deceived innocent"—or a "gullible fool"? Should she view herself as victim, or as co-conspirator in a shared delusion? Her husband is—what? An unsatisfied lover? A target of seduction? A psychopathic liar? The very Devil himself? *How could he be so cruel?* How could anyone? What is this home she has been living in? How could she be so naïve? How could anyone? She looks in the mirror. *Who is she? What's going on?* Are any of her relationships real? Have any of them ever been? What has happened to the future? Everything is up for grabs, when the deeper realities of the world unexpectedly manifest themselves.

Everything is intricate beyond imagining. Everything is affected by everything else. We perceive a very narrow slice of a causally interconnected matrix, although we strive with all our might to avoid being confronted by knowledge of that narrowness. The thin veneer of perceptual sufficiency cracks, however, when something fundamental goes wrong. The dreadful inadequacy of our senses reveals itself. Everything we hold dear crumbles to dust. We freeze. We turn to stone. What then do we see? Where can we look, when it is precisely what we see that has been insufficient?

What Do We See When We Don't Know What We're Looking At?

What is it, that is the world, after the Twin Towers disintegrate? What, if anything, is left standing? What dread beast rises from the ruins when the invisible pillars supporting the world's financial system tremble and fall? What do we see when we are swept up in the fire and drama of a National Socialist rally, or cower, paralyzed with fear, in the midst of a massacre in Rwanda? What is it that we see, when we cannot understand what is happening to us, cannot determine where we are, know no longer who we are, and no longer understand what surrounds us? What we *don't* see is the well-known and comforting world of tools—of useful objects—of personalities. We don't even see familiar obstacles—sufficiently troubling though they are in normal times, already mastered—that we can simply step around.

What we perceive, when things fall apart, is no longer the stage and settings of habitable order. It's the eternal watery *tohu va bohu*, formless emptiness, and the *tehom*, the abyss, to speak biblically—the chaos forever lurking beneath our thin surfaces of security. It's from that chaos that the Holy Word of God Himself extracted order at the beginning of time, according to the oldest opinions expressed by mankind (and it is in the image of that same Word that we were made, male and female, according to the same opinions). It's from that chaos that whatever stability we had the good fortune to experience emerged, originally—for some limited time—when we first learned to perceive. It's chaos that we see, when things fall apart (even though we cannot truly see it). What does all this mean?

Emergency—emergence(y). This is the sudden manifestation from somewhere unknown of some previously unknown phenomenon (from the Greek *phainesthai*, to "shine forth"). This is the reappearance of the eternal dragon, from its eternal cavern, from its now-disrupted slumber. This is the underworld, with its monsters rising from the depths. How do we prepare for an emergency, when we do not know what has emerged, or from where? How do we prepare for catastrophe, when we do not know what to expect, or how to act? We turn from our minds, so to speak—too slow, too ponderous— to our bodies. Our bodies react much faster than our minds.

When things collapse around us our perception disappears, and we act. Ancient reflexive responses, rendered automatic and efficient over hundreds of millions of years, protect us in those dire moments when not only thought but perception itself fails. Under such circumstances, our bodies ready themselves for all possible eventualities.[163] First, we freeze. The reflexes of the body then shade into emotion, the next stage of perception. Is this something scary? Something useful? Something that must be fought? Something that can be ignored? How will we determine this—and when? We don't know. Now we are in a costly and demanding state of readiness. Our bodies are flooded with cortisol and adrenaline. Our hearts beat faster. Our breath quickens. We realize, painfully, that our sense of competence and completeness is gone; it was just a dream. We draw on physical and psychological resources saved carefully for just this moment (if we are fortunate enough to have them). We prepare for the worst—or the best. We push the gas pedal furiously to the floor, and slam on the brakes at the same time. We scream, or laugh. We look disgusted, or terrified. We cry. And then we begin to parse apart the chaos.

And so, the deceived wife, increasingly unhinged, feels the motivation to reveal all—to herself, her sister, her best friend, to a stranger on a bus—or retreats into silence, and ruminates obsessively, to the same end. *What went wrong? What did she do that was so unforgivable? Who is this person she has been living with? What kind of world is this, where such things can happen? What kind of God would make such a place?* What conversation could she possibly initiate with this new, infuriating person, inhabiting the shell of her former husband? What forms of revenge might satisfy her anger? Who could she seduce, in return for this insult? She is by turns enraged, terrified, struck down by pain, and exhilarated by the possibilities of her new-found freedom.

Her last place of bedrock security was in fact not stable, not certain—not bedrock at all. Her house was built on a foundation of sand. The ice she was skating on was simply too thin. She fell through, into the water below, and is drowning. She has been hit so hard that her anger, terror and grief consume her. Her sense of betrayal widens, until the whole world caves in. Where is she? *In the underworld, with all its terrors.* How did she get there? This experience, this voyage into the substructure of things—this is all perception, too, in its nascent form; this preparation; this consideration of what-might-have-been and what-could-still-be; this emotion and fantasy. This is all the deep perception now necessary before the familiar objects that she once knew reappear, if they ever do, in their simplified and comfortable form. This is perception before the chaos of possibility is re-articulated into the functional realities of order.

"Was it really so unexpected?" she asks herself—she asks others—thinking back. Should she now feel guilty about ignoring the warning signs, subtle though they may have been, encouraged though she was to avoid them? She remembers when she first married, eagerly joining her husband, every single night, to make love. Perhaps that was too much to expect—or even too much to cope with—but once, in the last six months? Once every two or three months, for years, before that? Would anyone she could truly respect—including herself—put up with such a situation?

There is a story for children, *There's No Such Thing as a Dragon*, by Jack Kent, that I really like. It's a very simple tale, at least on the surface. I once read its few pages to a group of retired University of Toronto alumni, and explained its symbolic meaning. [fn2] It's about a small boy, Billy Bixbee, who spies a dragon sitting on his bed one morning. It's about the size of a house cat, and friendly. He tells his mother about it, but she tells him that there's no such thing as a dragon. So, it starts to grow. It eats all of Billy's pancakes. Soon it fills the whole house. Mom tries to vacuum, but she has to go in and out of the house through the windows because of the dragon everywhere. It takes her forever. Then, the dragon runs off with the house. Billy's dad comes home—and there's just an empty space, where he used to live. The mailman tells him where the house went. He chases after it, climbs up the dragon's head and neck (now sprawling out into the street) and rejoins his wife and son. Mom still insists that the dragon does not exist, but Billy, who's pretty much had it by now, insists, "There is a dragon, Mom." Instantly, it starts to shrink. Soon, it's cat-sized again. Everyone agrees that dragons of that size (1) exist and (2) are much preferable to their gigantic counterparts. Mom, eyes reluctantly opened by this point, asks somewhat plaintively why it had to get so big. Billy quietly suggests: "maybe it wanted to be noticed."

Maybe! That's the moral of many, many stories. Chaos emerges in a household, bit by bit. Mutual unhappiness and resentment pile up. Everything untidy is swept under the rug, where the dragon feasts on the crumbs. But no one says anything, as the shared society and negotiated order of the household reveals itself as inadequate, or disintegrates, in the face of the unexpected and threatening. Everybody whistles in the dark, instead. Communication would require admission of terrible emotions: resentment, terror, loneliness, despair, jealousy, frustration, hatred, boredom. Moment by moment, it's easier to keep the peace. But in the background, in Billy Bixbee's house, and in all that are like it, the dragon grows. One day it bursts forth, in a form that no one can ignore. It lifts the very household from its foundations. Then it's an affair, or a decades-long custody dispute of ruinous economic and psychological proportions. Then it's the concentrated version of the acrimony that could have been spread out, tolerably, issue by issue, over the years of the pseudo-paradise of the marriage. Every one of the three hundred thousand unrevealed issues, which have been lied about, avoided, rationalized away, hidden like an army of skeletons in some great horrific closet, bursts forth like Noah's flood, drowning everything. There's no ark, because no one built one, even though everyone felt the storm gathering.

Don't ever underestimate the destructive power of sins of omission.

Maybe the demolished couple could have had a conversation, or two, or two hundred, about their sex lives. Maybe the physical intimacy they undoubtedly shared should have been matched, as it often is not, *by a corresponding psychological intimacy*. Maybe they could have fought through their roles. In many households, in recent decades, the traditional household division of labour has been demolished, not least in the name of liberation and freedom. That demolition, however, has not left so much glorious lack of restriction in its wake as chaos, conflict and indeterminacy. The escape from tyranny is often followed not by Paradise, but by a sojourn in the desert, aimless, confused and deprived. Furthermore, in the absence of agreed-upon tradition (and the constraints—often uncomfortable; often even unreasonable—that it imposes) there exist only three difficult options: slavery, tyranny or negotiation. The slave merely does what he or she is told —happy, perhaps, to shed the responsibility—and solves the problem of complexity in that manner. But it's a temporary solution. The spirit of the slave rebels. The tyrant merely tells the slave what to do, and solves the problem of complexity in that manner. But it's a temporary solution. The tyrant tires of the slave. There's nothing and no one there, except for predictable and sullen obedience. Who can live forever with that? But negotiation—that requires forthright admission on the part of both players that the dragon exists. That's a reality difficult to face, even when it's still too small to simply devour the knight who dares confront it.

Maybe the demolished couple could have more precisely specified their desired manner of Being. Maybe in that manner they could have jointly prevented the waters of chaos from springing uncontrollably forth and drowning them. Maybe they could have done that instead of saying, in the agreeable, lazy and cowardly way: "It's OK. It's not worth fighting about." There is little, in a marriage, that is so little that it is not worth fighting about. You're stuck in a marriage like the two proverbial cats in a barrel, bound by the oath that lasts in theory until one or both of you die. That oath is there to make you take the damn situation seriously. Do you really want the same petty annoyance tormenting you every single day of your marriage, for the decades of its existence?

"Oh, I can put up with it," you think. And maybe you should. You're no paragon of genuine tolerance. And maybe if you brought up how your partner's giddy laugh is beginning to sound like nails on a blackboard he (or she) would tell you, quite properly, to go to hell. And maybe the fault is with you, and you should grow up, get yourself together and keep quiet. But perhaps braying like a donkey in the midst of a social gathering is not reflecting well on your partner, and you should stick to your guns. Under such circumstances, there is nothing but a fight—a fight with peace as the goal—that will reveal the truth. But you remain silent, and you convince yourself it's because you are a good, peace-loving, patient person (and nothing could be further from the truth). And the monster under the rug gains a few more pounds.

Maybe a forthright conversation about sexual dissatisfaction might have been the proverbial stitch in time—not that it would be easy. Perhaps *madame* desired the death of intimacy, clandestinely, because she was deeply and secretly ambivalent about sex. God knows there's reason to be. Perhaps *monsieur* was a terrible, selfish lover. Maybe they both were. Sorting that out is worth a fight, isn't it? That's a big part of life, isn't it? Perhaps addressing that and (you never know) solving the problem would be worth two months of pure misery just telling each other the truth (not with intent to destroy, or attain victory, because that's not the truth: that's just all-out war).

Maybe it wasn't sex. Maybe every conversation between husband and wife had deteriorated into boring routine, as no shared adventure animated the couple. Maybe that deterioration was easier, moment by moment, day by day, than bearing the responsibility of keeping the relationship alive. Living things die, after all, without attention. Life is indistinguishable from effortful maintenance. No one finds a match so perfect that the need for continued attention and work vanishes (and, besides, if you found the perfect person, he or she would run away from ever-so-imperfect you in justifiable horror). In truth, what you need—what you deserve, after all—is someone exactly as imperfect as you.

Maybe the husband who betrayed his wife was appallingly immature and selfish. Maybe that selfishness got the upper hand. Maybe she did not oppose this tendency with enough force and vigour. Maybe she could not agree with him on the proper disciplinary approach to the children, and shut him out of their lives, in consequence. Maybe that allowed him to circumvent what he saw as an unpleasant responsibility. Maybe hatred brewed in the hearts of the children, watching this underground battle, punished by the resentment of their mother and alienated, bit by bit, from good old Dad. Maybe the dinners she prepared for him—or he for her—were cold and bitterly eaten. Maybe all that unaddressed conflict left both resentful, in a manner unspoken, but effectively enacted. Maybe all that unspoken trouble started to undermine the invisible networks that supported the marriage. Maybe respect slowly turned into contempt, and no one deigned to notice. Maybe love slowly turned into hate, without mention.

Everything clarified and articulated becomes visible; maybe neither wife nor husband wished to see or understand. Maybe they left things purposefully in the fog. Maybe they generated the fog, to hide what they did not want to see. What did missus gain, when she turned from mistress to maid or mother? Was it a relief when her sex life disappeared? Could she complain more profitably to the neighbours and her mother when her husband turned away? Maybe that was more gratifying, secretly, than anything good that could be derived from any marriage, no matter how perfect. What can possibly compare to the pleasures of sophisticated and well-practised martyrdom? "She's such a saint, and married to such a terrible man. She deserved much better." That's a gratifying myth to live by, even if unconsciously chosen (the truth of the situation be damned). Maybe she never really liked her husband. Maybe she never really liked men, and still doesn't. Maybe that was her mother's fault—or her grandmother's. Maybe she mimicked their behaviour, acting out their trouble, transmitted unconsciously, implicitly, down the generations. Maybe she was taking revenge on her father, or her brother, or society.

What did her husband gain, for his part, when his sex life at home died? Did he willingly play along, as martyr, and complain bitterly to his friends? Did he use it as the excuse he wanted anyway to search for a new lover? Did he use it to justify the resentment he still felt towards women, in general, for the rejections he had faced so continuously before falling into his marriage?

Did he seize the opportunity to get effortlessly fat and lazy because he wasn't desired, in any case?

Maybe both, wife and husband alike, used the opportunity to mess up their marriage to take revenge upon God (perhaps the one Being who could have sorted through the mess).

Here's the terrible truth about such matters: every single voluntarily unprocessed and uncomprehended and ignored reason for marital failure will compound and conspire and will then plague that betrayed and self-betrayed woman for the rest of her life. The same goes for her husband. All she—he—they—or we—must do to ensure such an outcome *is nothing*: *don't notice, don't react, don't attend, don't discuss, don't consider, don't work for peace, don't take responsibility.* Don't confront the chaos and turn it into order—just wait, anything but naïve and innocent, for the chaos to rise up and engulf you instead.

Why avoid, when avoidance necessarily and inevitably poisons the future? Because the possibility of a monster lurks underneath all disagreements and errors. Maybe the fight you are having (or not having) with your wife or your husband signifies the beginning of the end of your relationship. Maybe your relationship is ending *because you are a bad person*. It's likely, at least in part. Isn't it? Having the argument necessary to solve a real problem therefore necessitates willingness to confront two forms of miserable and dangerous potential simultaneously: chaos (the potential fragility of the relationship—of all relationships—of life itself) and Hell (the fact that you—and your partner—could each be the person bad enough to ruin everything with your laziness and spite). There's every motivation to avoid. But it doesn't help.

Why remain vague, when it renders life stagnant and murky? Well, if you don't know who you are, you can hide in doubt. Maybe you're *not* a bad, careless, worthless person. Who knows? Not you. Particularly if you refuse to think about it—and you have every reason not to. But not thinking about something you don't want to know about doesn't make it go away. You are merely trading specific, particular, pointed knowledge of the likely finite list of your real faults and flaws for a much longer list of undefined potential inadequacies and insufficiencies.

Why refuse to investigate, when knowledge of reality enables mastery of reality (and if not mastery, at least the stature of an honest amateur)? Well, what if there truly is something rotten in the state of Denmark? Then what? Isn't it better under such conditions to live in willful blindness and enjoy the bliss of ignorance? Well, not if the monster is real! Do you truly think it is a good idea to retreat, to abandon the possibility of arming yourself against the rising sea of troubles, and to thereby diminish yourself in your own eyes? Do you truly think it wise to let the catastrophe grow in the shadows, while you shrink and decrease and become ever more afraid? Isn't it better to prepare, to sharpen your sword, to peer into the darkness, and then to beard the lion in its den? Maybe you'll get hurt. *Probably* you'll get hurt. Life, after all, is suffering. But maybe the wound won't be fatal.

If you wait instead until what you are refusing to investigate comes a-knocking at your door, things will certainly not go so well for you. What you least want will inevitably happen—and when you are least prepared. What you least want to encounter will make itself manifest when you are weakest and it is strongest. And you will be defeated.

> *Turning and turning in the widening gyre*
> *The falcon cannot hear the falconer;*
> *Things fall apart; the centre cannot hold;*
> *Mere anarchy is loosed upon the world,*
> *The blood-dimmed tide is loosed, and everywhere*
> *The ceremony of innocence is drowned;*
> *The best lack all conviction, while the worst*
>
> *Are full of passionate intensity.*[164]
> (William Butler Yeats, "The Second Coming")

Why refuse to specify, when specifying the problem would enable its solution? Because to specify the problem is to admit that it exists. Because to specify the problem is to allow yourself to know what you want, say, from friend or lover—and then you will know, precisely and cleanly, when you don't get it, and that will hurt, sharply and specifically. But you will learn something from that, and use what you learn in the future—and the alternative to that single sharp pain is the dull ache of continued hopelessness and vague failure and the sense that time, precious time, is slipping by.

Why refuse to specify? Because while you are failing to define success (and thereby rendering it impossible) you are also refusing to define failure, to yourself, so that if and when you fail you won't notice, and it won't hurt. But that won't work! You cannot be fooled so easily—unless you have gone very far down the road! You will instead carry with you a continual sense of disappointment in your own Being and the self-contempt that comes along with that and the increasing hatred for the world that all of that generates (or degenerates).

> *Surely some revelation is at hand;*
> *Surely the Second Coming is at hand.*
> *The Second Coming! Hardly are those words out*
> *When a vast image out of Spiritus Mundi*
> *Troubles my sight: somewhere in sands of the desert*
> *A shape with lion body and the head of a man,*
> *A gaze blank and pitiless as the sun,*
> *Is moving its slow thighs, while all about it*
> *Reel shadows of the indignant desert birds.*
> *The darkness drops again; but now I know*
> *That twenty centuries of stony sleep*
> *Were vexed to nightmare by a rocking cradle,*
> *And what rough beast, its hour come round at last,*
> *Slouches towards Bethlehem to be born?*

What if she who has been betrayed, now driven by desperation, is now determined to face all the incoherence of past, present and future? What if she decided to sort through the mess, even though she has avoided doing so until now, and is all the weaker and more confused for it? Perhaps the effort will nearly kill her (but she is now on a path worse than death in any case). To re-emerge, to escape, to be reborn, she must thoughtfully articulate the reality she comfortably but dangerously left hidden behind a veil of ignorance and the pretence of peace. She must separate the particular details of her specific catastrophe from the intolerable general condition of Being, in a world where everything has fallen apart. Everything—that's far too much. It was *specific* things that fell apart, not everything; *identifiable beliefs* failed; *particular actions* were false and inauthentic. What were they? How can they be fixed, now? How can she be better, in the future? She will never return to dry land if she refuses or is unable to figure it all out. She can put the world back together by some precision of thought, some precision of speech, some reliance on her word, some reliance on the Word. But perhaps it's better to leave things in the fog. Perhaps by now there just isn't enough left of her— perhaps too much of her has been left unrevealed, undeveloped. Maybe she simply no longer has the energy….

Some earlier care and courage and honesty in expression might have saved her from all this trouble. What if she had communicated her unhappiness with the decline of her romantic life, right when it started to decline? Precisely, exactly, when that decline first bothered her? Or, if it didn't bother her—what if she had instead communicated the fact it didn't bother her as much as it perhaps should have? What if she had clearly and carefully confronted the fact of our husband's contempt for her household efforts? Would she have discovered her resentment of her father and society itself (and the consequent contamination of her relationships)? What if she had fixed all that? How much stronger would she then have become? How much less likely to avoid facing up to difficulties, in consequence? How might she then have served herself, her family, and the world?

What if she had continually and honestly risked conflict in the present, in the service of longer-term truth and peace? What if she had treated the micro-collapses of her marriage as evidence of an underlying instability, eminently worthy of attention, instead of ignoring them, putting up with them, or smiling through them, in such a nice, agreeable manner? Maybe she would be different, and her husband, different too. Maybe they would still be married, formally and in spirit. Maybe they would both be much younger, physically and mentally, than they are now. Maybe her house would have been founded more on rock and less on sand.

When things fall apart, and chaos re-emerges, we can give structure to it, and re-establish order, through our speech. If we speak carefully and precisely, we can sort things out, and put them in their proper place, and set a new goal, and navigate to it—often communally, if we negotiate; if we reach consensus. If we speak carelessly and imprecisely, however, things remain vague. The destination remains unproclaimed. The fog of uncertainty does not lift, and there is no negotiating through the world.

The Construction of Soul and World

The psyche (the soul) and the world are both organized, at the highest levels of human existence, with language, through communication. Things are not as they appear when the outcome has been neither intended nor desired. Being has not been sorted into its proper categories, when it is not behaving. When something goes wrong, even perception itself must be questioned, along with evaluation, thought and action. When error announces itself, undifferentiated chaos is at hand. Its reptilian form paralyzes and confuses.

But dragons, which do exist (perhaps more than anything else exists) also hoard gold. In that collapse into the terrible mess of uncomprehended Being lurks the possibility of new and benevolent order. Clarity of thought—courageous clarity of thought—is necessary to call it forth.

The problem itself must be admitted to, as close to the time of its emergence as possible. "I'm unhappy," is a good start (not "I have a right to be unhappy," because that is still questionable, at the beginning of the problem-solving process). Perhaps your unhappiness is justified, under the current circumstances. Perhaps any reasonable person would be displeased and miserable to be where you are. Alternatively, perhaps, you are just whiny and immature? Consider both at least equally probable, as terrible as such consideration might appear. Just exactly how immature might you be? There's a potentially bottomless pit. But at least you might rectify it, if you can admit to it.

We parse the complex, tangled chaos, and specify the nature of things, including ourselves. It is in this way that our creative, communicative exploration continually generates and regenerates the world. We are shaped and informed by what we voluntarily encounter, and we shape what we inhabit, as well, in that encounter. This is difficult, but the difficulty is not relevant, because the alternative is worse.

Maybe our errant husband ignored the dinner conversation of his wife because he hated his job and was tired and resentful. Maybe he hated his job because his career was forced on him by his father and he was too weak or "loyal" to object. Maybe she put up with his lack of attention because she believed that forthright objection itself was rude and immoral. Maybe she hated her own father's anger and decided, when very young, that all aggression and assertiveness were morally wrong. Maybe she thought her husband wouldn't love her if she had any opinions of her own. It is very difficult to put such things in order—but damaged machinery will continue to malfunction if its problems are neither diagnosed nor fixed.

Wheat from Chaff

Precision specifies. When something terrible happens, it is precision that separates the unique terrible thing that has actually happened from all the other, equally terrible things that might have happened—but did not. If you wake up in pain, you might be dying. You might be dying slowly and terribly from one of a diverse number of painful, horrible diseases. If you refuse to tell your doctor about your pain, then what you have is unspecified: it could be *any* of those diseases—and it certainly (since you have avoided the diagnostic conversation—the act of articulation) is something unspeakable. But if you talk to your doctor, all those terrible possible diseases will collapse, with luck, into just one terrible (or not so terrible) disease, or even into nothing. Then you can laugh at your previous fears, and if something really is wrong, well, you're prepared. Precision may leave the tragedy intact, but it chases away the ghouls and the demons.

What you hear in the forest but cannot see might be a tiger. It might even be a conspiracy of tigers, each hungrier and more vicious than the other, led by a crocodile. But it might not be, too. If you turn and look, perhaps you'll see that it's just a squirrel. (I know someone who was actually chased by a squirrel.) Something is out there in the woods. You know that with certainty. But often it's only a squirrel. If you refuse to look, however, then it's a dragon, and you're no knight: you're a mouse confronting a lion; a rabbit, paralyzed by the gaze of a wolf. And I am not saying that it's always a squirrel. Often it's something truly terrible. But even what is terrible in actuality often pales in significance compared to what is terrible in imagination. And often what cannot be confronted because of its horror in imagination can in fact be confronted when reduced to its-still-admittedly-terrible actuality.

If you shirk the responsibility of confronting the unexpected, even when it appears in manageable doses, reality itself will become unsustainably disorganized and chaotic. Then it will grow bigger and swallow all order, all sense, and all predictability. Ignored reality transforms itself (reverts back) into the great Goddess of Chaos, the great reptilian Monster of the Unknown —the great predatory beast against which mankind has struggled since the dawn of time. If the gap between pretence and reality goes unmentioned, it will widen, you will fall into it, and the consequences will not be good. Ignored reality manifests itself in an abyss of confusion and suffering.

Be careful with what you tell yourself and others about what you have done, what you are doing, and where you are going. Search for the correct words. Organize those words into the correct sentences, and those sentences into the correct paragraphs. The past can be redeemed, when reduced by precise language to its essence. The present can flow by without robbing the future if its realities are spoken out clearly. With careful thought and language, the singular, stellar destiny that justifies existence can be extracted from the multitude of murky and unpleasant futures that are far more likely to manifest themselves of their own accord. This is how the Eye and the Word make habitable order.

Don't hide baby monsters under the carpet. They will flourish. They will grow large in the dark. Then, when you least expect it, they will jump out and devour you. You will descend into an indeterminate, confusing hell, instead of ascending into the heaven of virtue and clarity. Courageous and truthful words will render your reality simple, pristine, well-defined and habitable.

If you identify things, with careful attention and language, you bring them forward as viable, obedient objects, detaching them from their underlying near-universal interconnectedness. You simplify them. You make them specific and useful, and reduce their complexity. You make it possible to live with them and use them without dying from that complexity, with its attendant uncertainty and anxiety. If you leave things vague, then you'll never know what is one thing and what is another. Everything will bleed into everything else. This makes the world too complex to be managed.

You have to consciously define the topic of a conversation, particularly when it is difficult—or it becomes about everything, and everything is too much. This is so frequently why couples cease communicating. Every argument degenerates into every problem that ever emerged in the past, every problem that exists now, and every terrible thing that is likely to happen in the future. No one can have a discussion about "everything." Instead, you can say, "This exact, precise thing—that is what is making me unhappy. This exact, precise thing—that is what I want, as an alternative (although I am open to suggestions, if they are specific). This exact, precise thing—that is what you could deliver, so that I will stop making your life and mine miserable." But to do that, you have to *think*: What is wrong, *exactly*? What do I want, *exactly*? You must speak forthrightly and call forth the habitable world from chaos. You must use honest precise speech to do that. If instead you shrink away and hide, what you are hiding from will transform itself into the giant dragon that lurks under your bed and in your forest and in the dark recesses of your mind—and it will devour you.

You must determine where you have been in your life, so that you can know where you are now. If you don't know where you are, precisely, then you could be anywhere. Anywhere is too many places to be, and some of those places are very bad. You must determine where you have been in your life, because otherwise you can't get to where you're going. You can't get from point A to point B unless you are already at point A, and if you're just "anywhere" the chances you are at point A are very small indeed.

You must determine where you are going in your life, because you cannot get there unless you move in that direction. Random wandering will not move you forward. It will instead disappoint and frustrate you and make you anxious and unhappy and hard to get along with (and then resentful, and then vengeful, and then worse).

Say what you mean, so that you can find out what you mean. Act out what you say, so you can find out what happens. Then pay attention. Note your errors. Articulate them. Strive to correct them. That is how you discover the meaning of your life. That will protect you from the tragedy of your life. How could it be otherwise?

Confront the chaos of Being. Take aim against a sea of troubles. Specify your destination, and chart your course. Admit to what you want. Tell those around you who you are. Narrow, and gaze attentively, and move forward, forthrightly.

Be precise in your speech.

DO NOT BOTHER CHILDREN WHEN THEY ARE SKATEBOARDING

DANGER AND MASTERY

There was a time when kids skateboarded on the west side of Sidney Smith Hall, at the University of Toronto, where I work. Sometimes I stood there and watched them. There are rough, wide, shallow concrete steps there, leading up from the street to the front entrance, accompanied by tubular iron handrails, about two and a half inches in diameter and twenty feet long. The crazy kids, almost always boys, would pull back about fifteen yards from the top of the steps. Then they would place a foot on their boards, and skate like mad to get up some speed. Just before they collided with the handrail, they would reach down, grab their board with a single hand and jump onto the top of the rail, boardsliding their way down its length, propelling themselves off and landing—sometimes, gracefully, still atop their boards, sometimes, painfully, off them. Either way, they were soon back at it.

Some might call that stupid. Maybe it was. But it was brave, too. I thought those kids were amazing. I thought they deserved a pat on the back and some honest admiration. Of course it was dangerous. Danger was the point. They wanted to triumph over danger. They would have been safer in protective equipment, but that would have ruined it. They weren't trying to be safe. They were trying to become competent—and it's competence that makes people as safe as they can truly be.

I wouldn't dare do what those kids were doing. Not only that, I couldn't. I certainly couldn't climb a construction crane, like a certain type of modern daredevil, evident on YouTube (and, of course, people who work on construction cranes). I don't like heights, although the twenty-five thousand feet to which airliners ascend is so high that it doesn't bother me. I have flown several times in a carbon fibre stunt plane—even doing a hammerhead roll—and that was OK, although it's very physically and mentally demanding. (To perform a hammerhead roll, you pilot the plane straight up vertically, until the force of gravity makes it stall. Then it falls backwards, corkscrewing, until eventually it flips and noses straight down, after which you pull out of the dive. Or you don't do another hammerhead roll.) But I can't skateboard—especially down handrails—and I can't climb cranes.

Sidney Smith Hall faces another street on the east side. Along that street, named St. George—ironically enough—the university installed a series of rough, hard-edged, concrete plant boxes, sloping down to the roadway. The kids used to go out there, too, and boardslide along the box edges, as they did along the concrete surround of a sculpture adjacent to the building. That didn't last very long. Little steel brackets known as "skatestoppers" soon appeared, every two or three feet, along those edges. When I first saw them, I remembered something that happened in Toronto several years previously. Two weeks before elementary school classes started, throughout the city, all the playground equipment disappeared. The legislation governing such things had changed, and there was a panic about insurability. The playgrounds were hastily removed, even though they were sufficiently safe, grandfathered re their insurability, and often paid for (and quite recently) by parents. This meant no playgrounds at all for more than a year. During this time, I often saw bored but admirable kids charging around on the roof of our local school. It was that or scrounge about in the dirt with the cats and the less adventurous children.

I say "sufficiently safe" about the demolished playgrounds because when playgrounds are made too safe, kids either stop playing in them or start playing in unintended ways. Kids need playgrounds dangerous enough to remain challenging. People, including children (who are people too, after all) don't seek to minimize risk. They seek to optimize it. They drive and walk and love and play so that they achieve what they desire, but they push themselves a bit at the same time, too, so they continue to develop. Thus, if things are made too safe, people (including children) start to figure out ways to make them dangerous again.[165]

When untrammeled—and encouraged—we prefer to live on the edge. There, we can still be both confident in our experience and confronting the chaos that helps us develop. We're hard-wired, for that reason, to enjoy risk (some of us more than others). We feel invigorated and excited when we work to optimize our future performance, while playing in the present. Otherwise we lumber around, sloth-like, unconscious, unformed and careless. Overprotected, we will fail when something dangerous, unexpected and full of opportunity suddenly makes its appearance, as it inevitably will.

The skatestoppers are unattractive. The surround of the nearby sculpture would have to have been badly damaged by diligent boardsliders before it would look as mean as it does now, studded with metal like a pit bull's collar. The large plant boxes have metal guards placed at irregular intervals across their tops, and this, in addition to the wear caused by the skateboarders, produces a dismal impression of poor design, resentment and badly executed afterthoughts. It gives the area, which was supposed to be beautified by the sculpture and vegetation, a generic industrial/prison/mental institution/work-camp look of the kind that appears when builders and public officials do not like or trust the people they serve.

The sheer harsh ugliness of the solution makes a lie of the reasons for its implementation.

Success and Resentment

If you read the depth psychologists—Freud and Jung, for example, as well as their precursor, Friedrich Nietzsche—you learn that there is a dark side to everything. Freud delved deeply into the latent, implicit content of dreams, which were often aimed, in his opinion, at the expression of some improper wish. Jung believed that every act of social propriety was accompanied by its evil twin, its unconscious shadow. Nietzsche investigated the role played by what he termed *ressentiment* in motivating what were ostensibly selfless actions—and, often, exhibited all too publicly.[166]

> For that man be delivered from revenge—that is for me the bridge to the highest hope, and a rainbow after long storms. The tarantulas, of course, would have it otherwise. "What justice means to us is precisely that the world be filled with the storms of our revenge"—thus they speak to each other. "We shall wreak vengeange and abuse on all whose equals we are not"—thus do the tarantula-hearts vow. "And 'will to equality' shall henceforth be the name for virtue; and against all that has power we want to raise our clamor!" You preachers of equality, the tyrant-mania of impotence clamors thus out of you for equality: your most secret ambitions to be tyrants thus shroud themselves in words of virtue.

The incomparable English essayist George Orwell knew this sort of thing well. In 1937, he wrote *The Road to Wigan Pier*, which was in part a scathing attack on upper-class British socialists (this, despite being inclined towards socialism himself). In the first half of this book, Orwell portrays the appalling conditions faced by UK miners in the 1930s:[167]

> Several dentists have told me that in industrial districts a person over thirty with any of his or her own teeth is coming to be an abnormality. In Wigan various people gave me their opinion that it is best to get shut of your teeth as early in life as possible. 'Teeth is just a misery,' one woman said to me.

A Wigan Pier coal miner had to walk—crawl would be a better word, given the height of the mine shafts—up to three miles, underground, in the dark, banging his head and scraping his back, just to get to his seven-and-a-half-hour shift of backbreaking work. After that, he crawled back. "It is comparable, perhaps, to climbing a smallish mountain before and after your day's work," stated Orwell. None of the time spent crawling was paid.

Orwell wrote *The Road to Wigan Pier* for the Left Book Club, a socialist publishing group that released a select volume every month. After reading the first half of his book, which deals directly with the miners' personal circumstances, it is impossible not to feel sympathy for the working poor. Only a monster could keep his heart hardened through the accounts of the lives Orwell describes:

> It is not long since conditions in the mines were worse than they are now. There are still living a few very old women who in their youth have worked underground, crawling on all fours and dragging tubs of coal. They used to go on doing this even when they were pregnant.

In book's second half, however, Orwell turned his gaze to a different problem: the comparative unpopularity of socialism in the UK at the time, despite the clear and painful inequity observable everywhere. He concluded that the tweed-wearing, armchair-philosophizing, victim-identifying, pity-and-contempt-dispensing social-reformer types frequently did not like the poor, as they claimed. *Instead, they just hated the rich*. They disguised their resentment and jealousy with piety, sanctimony and self-righteousness. Things in the unconscious—or on the social justice–dispensing leftist front—haven't changed much, today. It is because of of Freud, Jung, Nietzsche—and Orwell—that I always wonder, "What, then, do you stand against?" whenever I hear someone say, too loudly, "I stand for this!" The question seems particularly relevant if the same someone is complaining, criticizing, or trying to change someone else's behaviour.

I believe it was Jung who developed the most surgically wicked of psychoanalytic dicta: *if you cannot understand why someone did something, look at the consequences—and infer the motivation.* This is a psychological scalpel. It's not always a suitable instrument. It can cut too deeply, or in the wrong places. It is, perhaps, a last-resort option. Nonetheless, there are times when its application proves enlightening.

If the consequences of placing skatestoppers on plant-boxes and sculpture bases, for example, is unhappy adolescent males and brutalist aesthetic disregard of beauty then, perhaps, that was the aim. When someone claims to be acting from the highest principles, for the good of others, there is no reason to assume that the person's motives are genuine. People motivated to make things better usually aren't concerned with changing other people—or, if they are, they take responsibility for making the same changes to themselves (and first). Beneath the production of rules stopping the skateboarders from doing highly skilled, courageous and dangerous things I see the operation of an insidious and profoundly anti-human spirit.

More about Chris

My friend Chris, whom I wrote about earlier, was possessed by such a spirit —to the serious detriment of his mental health. Part of what plagued him was guilt. He attended elementary and junior high school in a number of towns, up in the frigid expanses of the northernmost Alberta prairie, prior to ending up in the Fairview I wrote about earlier. Fights with Native kids were a too-common part of his experience, during those moves. It's no overstatement to point out that such kids were, on average, rougher than the white kids, or that they were touchier (and they had their reasons). I knew this well from my own experience.

I had a rocky friendship with a Métis kid, Rene Heck, [fn1] when I was in elementary school. It was rocky because the situation was complex. There was a large cultural divide between Rene and me. His clothes were dirtier. He was rougher in speech and attitude. I had skipped a grade in school, and was, in addition, small for my age. Rene was a big, smart, good-looking kid, and he was tough. We were in grade six together, in a class taught by my father. Rene was caught chewing gum. "Rene," said my father, "spit that gum out. You look like a cow." "Ha, ha," I laughed, under my breath. "Rene the cow."

Rene might have been a cow, but there was nothing wrong with his hearing. "Peterson," he said, "after school—you're dead."

Earlier in the morning, Rene and I had arranged to see a movie that night at the local movie theatre, the Gem. It looked like that was off. In any case, the rest of the day passed, quickly and unpleasantly, as it does when threat and pain lurk. Rene was more than capable of giving me a good pounding. After school, I took off for the bike stands outside the school as fast as I could, but Rene beat me there. We circled around the bikes, him on one side, me on the other. We were characters in a "Keystone Cops" short. As long as I kept circling, he couldn't catch me, but my strategy couldn't work forever. I yelled out that I was sorry, but he wasn't mollified. His pride was hurt, and he wanted me to pay.

I crouched down and hid behind some bikes, keeping an eye on Rene. "Rene," I yelled, "I'm sorry I called you a cow. Let's quit fighting." He started to approach me again. I said, "Rene, I am sorry I said that. Really. And I still want to go to the movie with you." This wasn't just a tactic. I meant it. Otherwise what happened next would not have happened. Rene stopped circling. Then he stared at me. Then he broke into tears. Then he ran off. That was Native-white relationships in a nutshell, in our hard little town. We never did go to a movie together.

When my friend Chris got into it with Native kids, he wouldn't fight back. He didn't feel that his self-defence was morally justified, so he took his beatings. "We took their land," he later wrote. "That was wrong. No wonder they're angry." Over time, step by step, Chris withdrew from the world. It was partly his guilt. He developed a deep hatred for masculinity and masculine activity. He saw going to school or working or finding a girlfriend as part of the same process that had led to the colonization of North America, the horrible nuclear stalemate of the cold war, and the despoiling of the planet. He had read some books about Buddhism, and felt that negation of his own Being was ethically required, in the light of the current world situation. He came to believe that the same applied to others.

When I was an undergraduate, Chris was, for a while, one of my roommates. One late night we went to a local bar. We walked home, afterward. He started to snap the side-view mirrors off parked cars, one after the other. I said, "Quit that, Chris. What possible good is it going to do to make the people who own these cars miserable?" He told me that they were all part of the frenetic human activity that was ruining everything, and that they deserved whatever they got. I said that taking revenge on people who were just living normal lives was not going to help anything.

Years later, when I was in graduate school in Montreal, Chris showed up, for what was supposed to be a visit. He was aimless, however, and lost. He asked if I could help. He ended up moving in. I was married by then, living with my wife, Tammy, and our year-old daughter, Mikhaila. Chris had also been friends with Tammy back in Fairview (and held out hopes of more than friendship). That complicated the situation even more—but not precisely in the manner you might think. Chris started by hating men, but he ended by hating women. He wanted them, but he had rejected education, and career, and desire. He smoked heavily, and was unemployed. Unsurprisingly, therefore, he was not of much interest to women. That made him bitter. I tried to convince him that the path he had chosen was only going to lead to further ruin. He needed to develop some humility. He needed to get a life.

One evening, it was Chris's turn to make dinner. When my wife came home, the apartment was filled with smoke. Hamburgers were burning furiously in the frying pan. Chris was on his hands and knees, attempting to repair something that had come loose on the legs of the stove. My wife knew his tricks. She knew he was burning dinner on purpose. He resented having to make it. He resented the feminine role (even though the household duties were split in a reasonable manner; even though he knew that perfectly well). He was fixing the stove to provide a plausible, even creditable excuse for burning the food. When she pointed out what he was doing, he played the victim, but he was deeply and dangerously furious. Part of him, and not the good part, was convinced that he was smarter than anyone else. It was a blow to his pride that she could see through his tricks. It was an ugly situation.

Tammy and I took a walk up towards a local park the next day. We needed to get away from the apartment, although it was thirty-five below—bitterly, frigidly cold, humid and foggy. It was windy. It was hostile to life. Living with Chris was too much, Tammy said. We entered the park. The trees forked their bare branches upward through the damp grey air. A black squirrel, tail hairless from mange, gripped a leafless branch, shivered violently, struggling to hold on against the wind. What was it doing out there in the cold? Squirrels are partial hibernators. They only come out in the winter when it's warm. Then we saw another, and another, and another, and another, and another. There were squirrels all around us in the park, all partially hairless, tails and bodies alike, all windblown on their branches, all shaking and freezing in the deathly cold. No one else was around. It was impossible. It was inexplicable. It was exactly appropriate. We were on the stage of an absurdist play. It was directed by God. Tammy left soon after with our daughter for a few days elsewhere.

Near Christmas time, that same year, my younger brother and his new wife came out to visit from western Canada. My brother also knew Chris. They all put on their winter clothes in preparation for a walk around downtown Montreal. Chris put on a long dark winter coat. He pulled a black toque, a brimless knitted cap, far down over his head. His coat was black, as were his pants and boots. He was very tall, and thin, and somewhat stooped. "Chris," I joked. "You look like a serial killer." Ha bloody ha. The three came back from their walk. Chris was out of sorts. There were strangers in his territory. Another happy couple. It was salt in his wounds.

We had dinner, pleasantly enough. We talked, and ended the evening. But I couldn't sleep. Something wasn't right. It was in the air. At four in the morning, I had had enough. I crawled out of bed. I knocked quietly on Chris's door and went without waiting for an answer into his room. He was awake on the bed, staring at the ceiling, as I knew he would be. I sat down beside him. I knew him very well. I talked him down from his murderous rage. Then I went back to bed, and slept. The next morning my brother pulled me aside. He wanted to speak with me. We sat down. He said, "What the hell was going on last night? I couldn't sleep at all. Was something wrong?" I told my brother that Chris wasn't doing so well. I didn't tell him that he was lucky to be alive—that we all were. The spirit of Cain had visited our house, but we were left unscathed.

Maybe I picked up some change in scent that night, when death hung in the air. Chris had a very bitter odour. He showered frequently, but the towels and the sheets picked up the smell. It was impossible to get them clean. It was the product of a psyche and a body that did not operate harmoniously. A social worker I knew, who also knew Chris, told me of her familiarity with that odour. Everyone at her workplace knew of it, although they only discussed it in hushed tones. They called it the smell of the unemployable.

Soon after this I finished my post-doctoral studies. Tammy and I moved away from Montreal to Boston. We had our second baby. Now and then,

Chris and I talked on the phone. He came to visit once. It went well. He had found a job at an auto-parts place. He was trying to make things better. He was OK at that point. But it didn't last. I didn't see him in Boston again. Almost ten years later—the night before Chris's fortieth birthday, as it happened—he called me again. By this time, I had moved my family to Toronto. He had some news. A story he had written was going to be published in a collection put together by a small but legitimate press. He wanted to tell me that. He wrote good short stories. I had read them all. We had discussed them at length. He was a good photographer, too. He had a good, creative eye. The next day, Chris drove his old pickup—the same battered beast from Fairview—into the bush. He ran a hose from the exhaust pipe into the front cab. I can see him there, looking through the cracked windshield, smoking, waiting. They found his body a few weeks later. I called his dad. "My beautiful boy," he sobbed.

Recently, I was invited to give a TEDx talk at a nearby university. Another professor talked first. He had been invited to speak because of his work—his genuinely fascinating, technical work—with computationally intelligent surfaces (like computer touchscreens, but capable of being placed everywhere). He spoke instead about the threat human beings posed to the survival of the planet. Like Chris—like far too many people—he had become anti-human, to the core. He had not walked as far down that road as my friend, but the same dread spirit animated them both.

He stood in front of a screen displaying an endless slow pan of a blocks-long Chinese high-tech factory. Hundreds of white-suited workers stood like sterile, inhuman robots behind their assembly lines, soundlessly inserting piece A into slot B. He told the audience—filled with bright young people—of the decision he and his wife had made to limit their number of children to one. He told them it was something they should all consider, if they wanted to regard themselves as ethical people. I felt that such a decision was properly considered—but only in his particular case (where less than one might have been even better). The many Chinese students in attendance sat stolidly through his moralizing. They thought, perhaps, of their parents' escape from the horrors of Mao's Cultural Revolution and its one-child policy. They thought, perhaps, of the vast improvement in living standard and freedom provided by the very same factories. A couple of them said as much in the question period that followed.

Would have the professor reconsidered his opinions, if he knew where such ideas can lead? I would like to say yes, but I don't believe it. I think he could have known, but refused to. Worse, perhaps: he knew, but didn't care —or knew, and was headed there, voluntarily, in any case.

Self-Appointed Judges of the Human Race

It has not been long since the Earth seemed infinitely larger than the people who inhabited it. It was only in the late 1800s that the brilliant biologist Thomas Huxley (1825-95)—staunch defender of Darwin and Aldous Huxley's grandfather—told the British Parliament that it was literally impossible for mankind to exhaust the oceans. Their power of generation was simply too great, as far as he could determine, compared to even the most assiduous human predations. It's been an even shorter fifty years since Rachel Carson's *Silent Spring* ignited the environmental movement.[168] Fifty years! That's nothing! That's not even yesterday.

We've only just developed the conceptual tools and technologies that allow us to understand the web of life, however imperfectly. We deserve a bit of sympathy, in consequence, for the hypothetical outrage of our destructive behaviour. Sometimes we don't know any better. Sometimes we do know better, but haven't yet formulated any practical alternatives. It's not as if life is easy for human beings, after all, even now—and it's only a few decades ago that the majority of human beings were starving, diseased and illiterate.[169] Wealthy as we are (increasingly, everywhere) we still only live decades that can be counted on our fingers. Even at present, it is the rare and fortunate family that does not contain at least one member with a serious illness—and all will face that problem eventually. We do what we can to make the best of things, in our vulnerability and fragility, and the planet is harder on us than we are on it. We could cut ourselves some slack.

Human beings are, after all, seriously remarkable creatures. We have no peers, and it's not clear that we have any real limits. Things happen now that appeared humanly impossible even at the same time in the recent past when we began to wake up to our planet-sized responsibilities. A few weeks before writing this I happened across two videos juxtaposed on YouTube. One showed the Olympic gold medal vault from 1956; the other, the Olympic silver medal vault from 2012. It didn't even look like the same sport—or the same animal. What McKayla Maroney did in 2012 would have been considered superhuman in the fifties. Parkour, a sport derived from French military obstacle course training, is amazing, as is free running. I watch compilations of such performances with unabashed admiration. Some of the kids jump off three-storey buildings without injury. It's dangerous—and amazing. Crane climbers are so brave it rattles the mind. The same goes for extreme mountain bikers, freestyle snowboarders, surfers of fifty-foot waves, and skateboarders.

The boys who shot up Columbine High School, whom we discussed earlier, had appointed themselves judges of the human race—like the TEDx professor, although much more extreme; like Chris, my doomed friend. For Eric Harris, the more literate of the two killers, human beings were a failed and corrupt species. Once a presupposition such as that is accepted, its inner logic will inevitably manifest itself. If something is a plague, as David Attenborough has it,[170] or a cancer, as the Club of Rome claimed,[171] the person who eradicates it is a hero—a veritable planetary saviour, in this case. A real messiah might follow through with his rigorous moral logic, and eliminate himself, as well. This is what mass murderers, driven by near-infinite resentment, typically do. Even their own Being does not justify the existence of humanity. In fact, they kill themselves precisely to demonstrate the purity of their commitment to annihilation. No one in the modern world may without objection express the opinion that existence would be bettered by the absence of Jews, blacks, Muslims, or Englishmen. Why, then, is it virtuous to propose that the planet might be better off, if there were fewer people on it? I can't help but see a skeletal, grinning face, gleeful at the possibility of the apocalypse, hiding not so very far behind such statements. And why does it so often seem to be the very people standing so visibly against prejudice who so often appear to feel obligated to denounce humanity itself?

I have seen university students, particularly those in the humanities, suffer genuine declines in their mental health from being philosophically berated by such defenders of the planet for their existence as members of the human species. It's worse, I think, for young men. As privileged beneficiaries of the patriarchy, their accomplishments are considered unearned. As possible adherents of rape culture, they're sexually suspect. Their ambitions make them plunderers of the planet. They're not welcome. At the junior high, high school and university level, they're falling behind educationally. When my son was fourteen, we discussed his grades. He was doing very well, he said, matter-of-factly, for a boy. I inquired further. Everyone knew, he said, that girls do better in school than boys. His intonation indicated surprise at my ignorance of something so self-evident. While writing this, I received the latest edition of *The Economist*. The cover story? "The Weaker Sex"—meaning males. In modern universities women now make up more than 50 percent of the students in more than two-thirds of all disciplines.

Boys are suffering, in the modern world. They are more disobedient—negatively—or more independent—positively—than girls, and they suffer for this, throughout their pre-university educational career. They are less agreeable (agreeableness being a personality trait associated with compassion, empathy and avoidance of conflict) and less susceptible to anxiety and depression,[172] at least after both sexes hit puberty.[173] Boys' interests tilt towards things; girls' interests tilt towards people.[174] Strikingly, these differences, strongly influenced by biological factors, are most pronounced in the Scandinavian societies where gender-equality has been pushed hardest: this is the opposite of what would be expected by those who insist, ever more loudly, that gender is a social construct. It isn't. This isn't a debate. The data are in.[175]

Boys like competition, and they don't like to obey, particularly when they are adolescents. During that time, they are driven to escape their families, and establish their own independent existence. There is little difference between doing that and challenging authority. Schools, which were set up in the late 1800s precisely to inculcate obedience,[176] do not take kindly to provocative and daring behaviour, no matter how tough-minded and competent it might show a boy (or a girl) to be. Other factors play their role in the decline of boys. Girls will, for example, play boys' games, but boys are much more reluctant to play girls' games. This is in part because it is admirable for a girl to win when competing with a boy. It is also OK for her to lose to a boy. For a boy to beat a girl, however, it is often not OK—and just as often, it is even less OK for him to lose. Imagine that a boy and a girl, aged nine, get into a fight. Just for engaging, the boy is highly suspect. If he wins, he's pathetic. If he loses—well, his life might as well be over. Beat up by a girl.

Girls can win by winning in their own hierarchy—by being good at what girls value, as girls. They can add to this victory by winning in the boys' hierarchy. Boys, however, can only win by winning in the male hierarchy. They will lose status, among girls *and* boys, by being good at what girls value. It costs them in reputation among the boys, and in attractiveness among the girls. Girls aren't attracted to boys who are their friends, even though they might like them, whatever that means. They are attracted to boys who win status contests with other boys. If you're male, however, you just can't hammer a female as hard as you would a male. Boys can't (won't) play truly competitive games with girls. It isn't clear how they can win. As the game turns into a girls' game, therefore, the boys leave. Are the universities —particularly the humanities—about to become a girls' game? Is this what we want?

The situation in the universities (and in educational institutions in general) is far more problematic than the basic statistics indicate.[177] If you eliminate the so-called STEM (science, technology, engineering and mathematics) programs (excluding psychology), the female/male ratio is even more skewed.[178] Almost 80 percent of students majoring in the fields of healthcare, public administration, psychology and education, which comprise one-quarter of all degrees, are female. The disparity is still rapidly increasing. At this rate, there will be very few men in most university disciplines in fifteen years. This is not good news for men. It might even be catastrophic news for men. But it's also not good news for women.

Career and Marriage

The women at female-dominated institutes of higher education are finding it increasingly difficult to arrange a dating relationship of even moderate duration. In consequence, they must settle, if inclined, for a hook-up, or sequential hook-ups. Perhaps this is a move forward, in terms of sexual liberation, but I doubt it. I think it's terrible for the girls.[179] A stable, loving relationship is highly desirable, for men as well as women. For women, however, it is often what is most wanted. From 1997 to 2012, according to the Pew Research Centre,[180] the number of women aged 18 to 34 who said that a successful marriage is one of the most important things in life rose from 28 to 37 percent (an increase of more than 30 percent [fn2]). The number of young men who said the same thing declined 15 percent over the same period (from 35 to 29 percent [fn3]). During that time, the proportion of married people over 18 continued to decline, down from three-quarters in 1960 to half now.[181] Finally, among never-married adults aged 30 to 59, men are three times as likely as women to say they do not ever want to marry (27 vs 8 percent).

Who decided, anyway, that career is more important than love and family? Is working eighty hours a week at a high-end law firm truly worth the sacrifices required for that kind of success? And if it is worth it, why is it worth it? A minority of people (mostly men, who score low in the trait of agreeableness, again) are hyper-competitive, and want to win at any cost. A minority will find the work intrinsically fascinating. But most aren't, and most won't, and money doesn't seem to improve people's lives, once they have enough to avoid the bill collectors. Furthermore, most high-performing and high-earning females have high-performing and high-earning partners— and that matters more to women. The Pew data also indicate that a spouse with a desirable job is a high priority for almost 80 percent of never-married but marriage-seeking women (but for less than 50 percent of men).

When they hit their thirties, most of the top-rate female lawyers bail out of their high-pressure careers.[182] Only 15 percent of equity partners at the two hundred biggest US law firms are women.[183] This figure hasn't changed much in the last fifteen years, even though female associates and staff attorneys are plentiful. It also isn't because the law firms don't want the women to stay around and succeed. There is a chronic shortage of excellent people, regardless of sex, and law firms are desperate to retain them.

The women who leave want a job—and a life—that allows them some time. After law school and articling and the few first years of work, they develop other interests. This is common knowledge in the big firms (although it is not something that people are comfortable articulating in public, men and women alike). I recently watched a McGill University professor, female, lecture a room full of female law partners or near-partners about how lack of childcare facilities and "male definitions of success" impeded their career progress and caused women to leave. I knew most of the women in the room. We had talked at great length. I knew they knew that none of this was at all the problem. They had nannies, and they could afford them. They had already outsourced all their domestic obligations and necessities. They understood, as well—and perfectly well—that it was the market that defined success, not the men they worked with. If you are earning $650 an hour in Toronto as a top lawyer, and your client in Japan phones you at 4 a.m. on a Sunday, you answer. Now. You answer, now, even if you have just gone back to sleep after feeding the baby. You answer because some hyper-ambitious legal associate in New York would be happy to answer, if you don't—and that's why the market defines the work.

The increasingly short supply of university-educated men poses a problem of increasing severity for women who want to marry, as well as date. First, women have a strong proclivity to marry across or up the economic dominance hierarchy. They prefer a partner of equal or greater status. This holds true cross-culturally.[184] The same does not hold, by the way, for men, who are perfectly willing to marry across or down (as the Pew data indicate), although they show a preference for somewhat younger mates. The recent trend towards the hollowing-out of the middle class has also been increasing as resource-rich women tend more and more[185] to partner with resource-rich men. Because of this, and because of the decline in high-paying manufacturing jobs for men (one of six men of employable age is currently without work in the US), marriage is now something increasingly reserved for the rich. I can't help finding that amusing, in a blackly ironic manner. The oppressive patriarchal institution of marriage has now become a luxury. Why would the rich tyrannize themselves?

Why do women want an employed partner and, preferably, one of higher status? In no small part, it's because women become more vulnerable when they have children. They need someone competent to support mother and child when that becomes necessary. It's a perfectly rational compensatory act, although it may also have a biological basis. Why would a woman who decides to take responsibility for one or more infants want an adult to look after as well? So, the unemployed working man is an undesirable specimen— and single motherhood an undesirable alternative. Children in father-absent homes are four times as likely to be poor. That means their mothers are poor too. Fatherless children are at much greater risk for drug and alcohol abuse. Children living with married biological parents are less anxious, depressed and delinquent than children living with one or more non-biological parent. Children in single-parent families are also twice as likely to commit suicide.[186]

The strong turn towards political correctness in universities has exacerbated the problem. The voices shouting against oppression have become louder, it seems, in precise proportion to how equal—even now increasingly skewed against men—the schools have become. There are whole disciplines in universities forthrightly hostile towards men. These are the areas of study, dominated by the postmodern/neo-Marxist claim that Western culture, in particular, is an oppressive structure, created by white men to dominate and exclude women (and other select groups); successful only because of that domination and exclusion.[187]

The Patriarchy: Help or Hindrance?

Of course, culture *is* an oppressive structure. *It's always been that way.* It's a fundamental, universal existential reality. The tyrannical king is a symbolic truth; an archetypal constant. What we inherit from the past is willfully blind, and out of date. It's a ghost, a machine, and a monster. It must be rescued, repaired and kept at bay by the attention and effort of the living. It crushes, as it hammers us into socially acceptable shape, and it wastes great potential. But it offers great gain, too. Every word we speak is a gift from our ancestors. Every thought we think was thought previously by someone smarter. The highly functional infrastructure that surrounds us, particularly in the West, is a gift from our ancestors: the comparatively uncorrupt political and economic systems, the technology, the wealth, the lifespan, the freedom, the luxury, and the opportunity. Culture takes with one hand, but in some fortunate places it gives more with the other. To think about culture only as oppressive is ignorant and ungrateful, as well as dangerous. This is not to say (as I am hoping the content of this book has made abundantly clear, so far) that culture should not be subject to criticism.

Consider this, as well, in regard to oppression: *any hierarchy creates winners and losers.* The winners are, of course, more likely to justify the hierarchy and the losers to criticize it. But (1) the collective pursuit of any valued goal produces a hierarchy (as some will be better and some worse at that pursuit not matter what it is) and (2) it is the pursuit of goals that in large part lends life its sustaining meaning. We experience almost all the emotions that make life deep and engaging as a consequence of moving successfully towards something deeply desired and valued. The price we pay for that involvement is the inevitable creation of hierarchies of success, while the inevitable consequence is difference in outcome. Absolute equality would therefore require the sacrifice of value itself—and then there would be nothing worth living for. We might instead note with gratitude that a complex, sophisticated culture allows for many games and many successful players, and that a well-structured culture allows the individuals that compose it to play and to win, in many different fashions.

It is also *perverse* to consider culture the creation of men. Culture is symbolically, archetypally, mythically male. That's partly why the idea of "the patriarchy" is so easily swallowed. But it is certainly the creation of humankind, not the creation of men (let alone white men, who nonetheless contributed their fair share). European culture has only been dominant, to the degree that it is dominant at all, for about four hundred years. On the time scale of cultural evolution—which is to be measured, at minimum, in thousands of years—such a timespan barely registers. Furthermore, even if women contributed nothing substantial to art, literature and the sciences prior to the 1960s and the feminist revolution (which is not something I believe), then the role they played raising children and working on the farms was still instrumental in raising boys and freeing up men—a very few men—so that humanity could propagate itself and strive forward.

Here's an alternative theory: throughout history, men and women both struggled terribly for freedom from the overwhelming horrors of privation and necessity. Women were often at a disadvantage during that struggle, as they had all the vulnerabilities of men, with the extra reproductive burden, and less physical strength. In addition to the filth, misery, disease, starvation, cruelty and ignorance that characterized the lives of both sexes, back before the twentieth century (when even people in the Western world typically existed on less than a dollar a day in today's money) women also had to put up with the serious practical inconvenience of menstruation, the high probability of unwanted pregnancy, the chance of death or serious damage during childbirth, and the burden of too many young children. Perhaps that is sufficient reason for the different legal and practical treatment of men and women that characterized most societies prior to the recent technological revolutions, including the invention of the birth control pill. At least such things might be taken into account, before the assumption that men tyrannized women is accepted as a truism.

It looks to me like the so-called oppression of the patriarchy was instead an imperfect collective attempt by men and women, stretching over millennia, to free each other from privation, disease and drudgery. The recent case of Arunachalam Muruganantham provides a salutary example. This man, the "tampon king" of India, became unhappy because his wife had to use dirty rags during her menstrual period. She told him it was either expensive sanitary napkins, or milk for the family. He spent the next fourteen years in a state of insanity, by his neighbours' judgment, trying to rectify the problem. Even his wife and his mother abandoned him, briefly, terrified as they became of his obsession. When he ran out of female volunteers to test his product, he took to wearing a bladder of pig's blood as a replacement. I can't see how this behaviour would have improved his popularity or status. Now his low-cost and locally made napkins are distributed across India, manufactured by women-run self-help groups. His users have been provided with freedom they never previously experienced. In 2014, this high-school dropout was named one of *Time* magazine's 100 most influential people in the world. I am unwilling to consider personal gain Muruganantham's primary motivation. Is he part of the patriarchy?

In 1847, James Young Simpson used ether to help a woman who had a deformed pelvis give birth. Afterwards, he switched to the better-performing chloroform. The first baby delivered under its influence was named "Anaesthesia." By 1853, chloroform was esteemed enough to be used by Queen Victoria, who delivered her seventh baby under its influence. Remarkably soon afterward, the option of painless childbirth was available everywhere. A few people warned of the danger of opposing God's pronouncement to women in Genesis 3:16: "I will greatly multiply thy sorrow and thy conception; in sorrow thou shalt bring forth children …" Some also opposed its use among males: young, healthy, courageous men simply did not need anaesthesia. Such opposition was ineffectual. Use of anaesthesia spread with extreme rapidity (and far faster than would be possible today). Even prominent churchmen supported its use.

The first practical tampon, Tampax, didn't arrive until the 1930s. It was invented by Dr. Earle Cleveland Haas. He made it of compressed cotton, and designed an applicator from paper tubes. This helped lessen resistance to the products by those who objected to the self-touching that might otherwise occur. By the early 1940s, 25 percent of women were using them. Thirty years later, it was 70 percent. Now it's four out of five, with the remainder relying on pads, which are now hyper-absorbent, and held in place by effective adhesives (opposed to the awkwardly placed, bulky, belted, diaper-like sanitary napkins of the 1970s). Did Muruganantham, Simpson and Haas oppress women, or free them? What about Gregory Goodwin Pincus, who invented the birth control pill? In what manner were these practical, enlightened, persistent men part of a constricting patriarchy?

Why do we teach our young people that our incredible culture is the result of male oppression? Blinded by this central assumption disciplines as diverse as education, social work, art history, gender studies, literature, sociology and, increasingly, law actively treat men as oppressors and men's activity as inherently destructive. They also often directly promote radical political action—radical by all the norms of the societies within which they are situated—which they do not distinguish from education. The Pauline Jewett Institute of Women's and Gender Studies at Ottawa's Carleton University, for example, encourages activism as part of their mandate. The Gender Studies Department at Queen's University in Kingston, Ontario, "teaches feminist, anti-racist, and queer theories and methods that centre activism for social change"—indicating support for the supposition that university education should above all foster political engagement of a particular kind.

Postmodernism and the Long Arm of Marx

These disciplines draw their philosophy from multiple sources. All are heavily influenced by the Marxist humanists. One such figure is Max Horkheimer, who developed critical theory in the 1930s. Any brief summary of his ideas is bound to be oversimplified, but Horkheimer regarded himself as a Marxist. He believed that Western principles of individual freedom or the free market were merely masks that served to disguise the true conditions of the West: inequality, domination and exploitation. He believed that intellectual activity should be devoted to social change, instead of mere understanding, and hoped to emancipate humanity from its enslavement. Horkheimer and his Frankfurt School of associated thinkers—first, in

Germany and later, in the US—aimed at a full-scale critique and transformation of Western civilization.

More important in recent years has been the work of French philosopher Jacques Derrida, leader of the postmodernists, who came into vogue in the late 1970s. Derrida described his own ideas as a radicalized form of Marxism. Marx attempted to reduce history and society to economics, considering culture the oppression of the poor by the rich. When Marxism was put into practice in the Soviet Union, China, Vietnam, Cambodia and elsewhere, economic resources were brutally redistributed. Private property was eliminated, and rural people forcibly collectivized. The result? Tens of millions of people died. Hundreds of millions more were subject to oppression rivalling that still operative in North Korea, the last classic communist holdout. The resulting economic systems were corrupt and unsustainable. The world entered a prolonged and extremely dangerous cold war. The citizens of those societies lived the life of the lie, betraying their families, informing on their neighbours—existing in misery, without complaint (or else).

Marxist ideas were very attractive to intellectual utopians. One of the primary architects of the horrors of the Khmer Rouge, Khieu Samphan, received a doctorate at the Sorbonne before he became the nominal head of Cambodia in the mid-1970s. In his doctoral thesis, written in 1959, he argued that the work done by non-farmers in Cambodia's cities was unproductive: bankers, bureaucrats and businessmen added nothing to society. Instead, they parasitized the genuine value produced through agriculture, small industry and craft. Samphan's ideas were favourably looked upon by the French intellectuals who granted him his Ph.D. Back in Cambodia, he was provided with the opportunity to put his theories into practice. The Khmer Rouge evacuated Cambodia's cities, drove all the inhabitants into the countryside, closed the banks, banned the use of currency, and destroyed all the markets. A quarter of the Cambodian population were worked to death in the countryside, in the killing fields.

Lest We Forget: Ideas Have Consequences.

When the communists established the Soviet Union after the First World War, people could be forgiven for hoping that the utopian collectivist dreams their new leaders purveyed were possible. The decayed social order of the late nineteenth century produced the trenches and mass slaughters of the Great War. The gap between rich and poor was extreme, and most people slaved away in conditions worse than those later described by Orwell. Although the West received word of the horror perpetrated by Lenin after the Russian Revolution, it remained difficult to evaluate his actions from afar. Russia was in post-monarchical chaos, and the news of widespread industrial development and redistribution of property to those who had so recently been serfs provided reason for hope. To complicate things further, the USSR (and Mexico) supported the democratic Republicans when the Spanish Civil War broke out, in 1936. They were fighting against the essentially fascist Nationalists, who had overthrown the fragile democracy established only five years previously, and who found support with the Nazis and Italian fascists.

The intelligentsia in America, Great Britain and elsewhere were severely frustrated by their home countries' neutrality. Thousands of foreigners streamed into Spain to fight for the Republicans, serving in the International Brigades. George Orwell was one of them. Ernest Hemingway served there as a journalist, and was a supporter of the Republicans. Politically concerned young Americans, Canadians and Brits felt a moral obligation to stop talking and start fighting.

All of this drew attention away from concurrent events in the Soviet Union. In the 1930s, during the Great Depression, the Stalinist Soviets sent two million kulaks, their richest peasants, to Siberia (those with a small number of cows, a couple of hired hands, or a few acres more than was typical). From the communist viewpoint, these kulaks had gathered their wealth by plundering those around them, and deserved their fate. Wealth signified oppression, and private property was theft. It was time for some equity. More than thirty thousand kulaks were shot on the spot. Many more met their fate at the hands of their most jealous, resentful and unproductive neighbours, who used the high ideals of communist collectivization to mask their murderous intent.

The kulaks were "enemies of the people," apes, scum, vermin, filth and swine. "We will make soap out of the kulak," claimed one particularly brutal cadre of city-dwellers, mobilized by party and Soviet executive committees, and sent out into the countryside. The kulaks were driven, naked, into the streets, beaten, and forced to dig their own graves. The women were raped.

Their belongings were "expropriated," which, in practice, meant that their houses were stripped down to the rafters and ceiling beams and everything was stolen. In many places, the non-kulak peasants resisted, particularly the women, who took to surrounding the persecuted families with their bodies. Such resistance proved futile. The kulaks who didn't die were exiled to Siberia, often in the middle of the night. The trains started in February, in the bitter Russian cold. Housing of the most substandard kind awaited them upon arrival on the desert taiga. Many died, particularly children, from typhoid, measles and scarlet fever.

The "parasitical" kulaks were, in general, the most skillful and hardworking farmers. A small minority of people are responsible for most of the production in any field, and farming proved no different. Agricultural output crashed. What little remained was taken by force out of the countryside and into the cities. Rural people who went out into the fields after the harvest to glean single grains of wheat for their hungry families risked execution. Six million people died of starvation in the Ukraine, the breadbasket of the Soviet Union, in the 1930s. "To eat your own children is a barbarian act," declared posters of the Soviet regime.

Despite more than mere rumours of such atrocities, attitudes towards communism remained consistently positive among many Western intellectuals. There were other things to worry about, and the Second World War allied the Soviet Union with the Western countries opposing Hitler, Mussolini and Hirohito. Certain watchful eyes remained open, nonetheless. Malcolm Muggeridge published a series of articles describing Soviet demolition of the peasantry as early as 1933, for the *Manchester Guardian*. George Orwell understood what was going on under Stalin, and he made it widely known. He published *Animal Farm*, a fable satirizing the Soviet Union, in 1945, despite encountering serious resistance to the book's release. Many who should have known better retained their blindness for long after this. Nowhere was this truer than France, and nowhere truer in France than among the intellectuals.

France's most famous mid-century philosopher, Jean-Paul Sartre, was a well-known communist, although not a card-carrier, until he denounced the Soviet incursion into Hungary in 1956. He remained an advocate for Marxism, nonetheless, and did not finally break with the Soviet Union until

1968, when the Soviets violently suppressed the Czechoslovakians during the Prague Spring.

Not long after came the publication of Aleksandr Solzhenitsyn's *The Gulag Archipelago*, which we have discussed rather extensively in previous chapters. As noted (and is worth noting again), this book utterly demolished communism's moral credibility—first in the West, and then in the Soviet System itself. It circulated in underground *samizdat* format. Russians had twenty-four hours to read their rare copy before handing it to the next waiting mind. A Russian-language reading was broadcast into the Soviet Union by Radio Liberty.

Solzhenitsyn argued that the Soviet system could have never survived without tyranny and slave labour; that the seeds of its worst excesses were definitively sowed in the time of Lenin (for whom the Western communists still served as apologists); and that it was propped up by endless lies, both individual and public. Its sins could not be blamed on a simple cult of personality, as its supporters continued to claim. Solzhenitsyn documented the Soviet Union's extensive mistreatment of political prisoners, its corrupt legal system, and its mass murders, and showed in painstaking detail how these were not aberrations but direct expressions of the underlying communist philosophy. No one could stand up for communism after *The Gulag Archipelago*—not even the communists themselves.

This did not mean that the fascination Marxist ideas had for intellectuals—particularly French intellectuals—disappeared. It merely transformed. Some refused outright to learn. Sartre denounced Solzhenitsyn as a "dangerous element." Derrida, more subtle, substituted the idea of power for the idea of money, and continued on his merry way. Such linguistic sleight-of-hand gave all the barely repentant Marxists still inhabiting the intellectual pinnacles of the West the means to retain their world-view. Society was no longer repression of the poor by the rich. It was oppression of everyone by the powerful.

According to Derrida, hierarchical structures emerged only to include (the beneficiaries of that structure) and to exclude (everyone else, who were therefore oppressed). Even that claim wasn't sufficiently radical. Derrida claimed that divisiveness and oppression were built right into language—built into the very categories we use to pragmatically simplify and negotiate the world. There are "women" only because men gain by excluding them.

There are "males and females" only because members of that more heterogeneous group benefit by excluding the tiny minority of people whose biological sexuality is amorphous. Science only benefits the scientists. Politics only benefits the politicians. In Derrida's view, hierarchies exist because they gain from oppressing those who are omitted. It is this ill-gotten gain that allows them to flourish.

Derrida famously said (although he denied it, later): "Il n'y a pas de hors-texte"—often translated as "there is nothing outside the text." His supporters say that is a mistranslation, and that the English equivalent should have been "there is no outside-text." It remains difficult, either way, to read the statement as saying anything other than "everything is interpretation," and that is how Derrida's work has generally been interpreted.

It is almost impossible to over-estimate the nihilistic and destructive nature of this philosophy. It puts the act of categorization itself in doubt. It negates the idea that distinctions might be drawn between things for any reasons other than that of raw power. Biological distinctions between men and women? Despite the existence of an overwhelming, multi-disciplinary scientific literature indicating that sex differences are powerfully influenced by biological factors, science is just another game of power, for Derrida and his post-modern Marxist acolytes, making claims to benefit those at the pinnacle of the scientific world. There are no facts. Hierarchical position and reputation as a consequence of skill and competence? All definitions of skill and of competence are merely made up by those who benefit from them, to exclude others, and to benefit personally and selfishly.

There is sufficient truth to Derrida's claims to account, in part, for their insidious nature. Power is a fundamental motivational force ("a," not "the"). People compete to rise to the top, and they care where they are in dominance hierarchies. But (and this is where you separate the metaphorical boys from the men, philosophically) *the fact that power plays a role in human motivation does not mean that it plays the only role, or even the primary role.* Likewise, the fact that we can never know everything does make all our observations and utterances dependent on taking some things into account and leaving other things out (as we discussed extensively in Rule 10). That does not justify the claim that everything is interpretation, or that categorization is just exclusion. Beware of single cause interpretations—and beware the people who purvey them.

Although the facts cannot speak for themselves (just as an expanse of land spread out before a voyager cannot tell him how to journey through it), and although there are a myriad ways to interact with—even to perceive—even a small number of objects, that does not mean that all interpretations are equally valid. Some hurt—yourself and others. Others put you on a collision course with society. Some are not sustainable across time. Others do not get you where you want to go. Many of these constraints are built in to us, as a consequence of billions of years of evolutionary processes. Others emerge as we are socialized into cooperating and competing peacefully and productively with others. Still more interpretations emerge as we discard counterproductive strategies through learning. An endless number of interpretations, certainly: that is not different than saying an endless number of problems. *But a seriously bounded number of viable solutions.* Otherwise life would be easy. And it's not.

Now, I have some beliefs that might be regarded as left-leaning. I think, for example, that the tendency for valuable goods to distribute themselves with pronounced inequality constitutes an ever-present threat to the stability of society. I think there is good evidence for that. That does not mean that the solution to the problem is self-evident. We don't know how to redistribute wealth without introducing a whole host of other problems. Different Western societies have tried different approaches. The Swedes, for example, push equality to its limit. The US takes the opposite tack, assuming that the net wealth-creation of a more free-for-all capitalism constitutes the rising tide that lifts all boats. The results of these experiments are not all in, and countries differ very much in relevant ways. Differences in history, geographic area, population size and ethnic diversity make direct comparisons very difficult. But it certainly is the case that forced redistribution, in the name of utopian equality, is a cure to shame the disease.

I think, as well (on what might be considered the leftish side), that the incremental remake of university administrations into analogues of private corporations is a mistake. I think that the science of management is a pseudo-discipline. I believe that government can, sometimes, be a force for good, as well as the necessary arbiter of a small set of necessary rules. Nonetheless, I do not understand why our society is providing public funding to institutions and educators whose stated, conscious and explicit aim is the demolition of the culture that supports them. Such people have a perfect right to their opinions and actions, if they remain lawful. But they have no reasonable claim to public funding. If radical right-wingers were receiving state funding for political operations disguised as university courses, as the radical left-wingers clearly are, the uproar from progressives across North America would be deafening.

There are other serious problems lurking in the radical disciplines, apart from the falseness of their theories and methods, and their insistence that collective political activism is morally obligatory. There isn't a shred of hard evidence to support any of their central claims: that Western society is pathologically patriarchal; that the prime lesson of history is that men, rather than nature, were the primary source of the oppression of women (rather than, as in most cases, their partners and supporters); that all hierarchies are based on power and aimed at exclusion. Hierarchies exist for many reasons—some arguably valid, some not—and are incredibly ancient, evolutionarily speaking. Do male crustaceans oppress female crustaceans? Should their hierarchies be upended?

In societies that are well-functioning—not in comparison to a hypothetical utopia, but contrasted with other existing or historical cultures—*competence,* not power, is a prime determiner of status. Competence. Ability. Skill. Not *power.* This is obvious both anecdotally and factually. No one with brain cancer is equity-minded enough to refuse the service of the surgeon with the best education, the best reputation and, perhaps, the highest earnings. Furthermore, the most valid personality trait predictors of long-term success in Western countries are intelligence (as measured with cognitive ability or IQ tests) and conscientiousness (a trait characterized by industriousness and orderliness).[188] There are exceptions. Entrepreneurs and artists are higher in openness to experience,[189] another cardinal personality trait, than in conscientiousness. But openness is associated with verbal intelligence and creativity, so that exception is appropriate and understandable. The predictive power of these traits, mathematically and economically speaking, is exceptionally high—among the highest, in terms of power, of anything ever actually measured at the harder ends of the social sciences. A good battery of personality/cognitive tests can increase the probability of employing someone more competent than average from 50:50 to 85:15. These are the facts, as well supported as anything in the social sciences (and this is saying more than you might think, as the social sciences are more effective disciplines than their cynical critics appreciate). Thus, not only is the state supporting one-sided radicalism, it is also supporting indoctrination. We do not teach our children that the world is flat. Neither should we teach them unsupported ideologically-predicated theories about the nature of men and women—or the nature of hierarchy.

It is not unreasonable to note (if the deconstructionists would leave it at that) that science can be biased by the interests of power, and to warn against that—or to point out that evidence is too often what powerful people, including scientists, decide it is. After all, scientists are people too, and people like power, just like lobsters like power—just like deconstructionists like to be known for their ideas, and strive rightly to sit atop their academic hierarchies. But that doesn't mean that science—or even deconstructionism—is only about power. Why believe such a thing? Why insist upon it? Perhaps it's this: *if only power exists, then the use of power becomes fully justifiable.* There is no bounding such use by evidence, method, logic, or even the necessity for coherence. There is no bounding by anything "outside the text." That leaves opinion—and force—and the use of force is all too attractive, under such circumstances, just as its employment in the service of that opinion is all too certain. The insane and incomprehensible postmodern insistence that all gender differences are socially constructed, for example, becomes all too understandable when its moral imperative is grasped—when its justification for force is once and for all understood: *Society must be altered, or bias eliminated, until all outcomes are equitable.* But the bedrock of the social constructionist position is the wish for the latter, not belief in the justice of the former. Since all outcome inequalities must be eliminated (inequality being the heart of all evil), then all gender differences must be regarded as socially constructed. Otherwise the drive for equality would be too radical, and the doctrine too blatantly propagandistic. Thus, the order of logic is reversed, so that the ideology can be camouflaged. The fact that such statements lead immediately to internal inconsistencies within the ideology is never addressed. Gender is constructed, but an individual who desires gender re-assignment surgery is to be unarguably considered a man trapped in a woman's body (or vice versa). *The fact that both of these cannot logically be true, simultaneously, is just ignored* (or rationalized away with another appalling post-modern claim: that logic itself—along with the techniques of science—is merely part of the oppressive patriarchal system).

It is also the case, of course, that all outcomes cannot be equalized. First, outcomes must be measured. Comparing the salaries of people who occupy the same position is relatively straightforward (although complicated significantly by such things as date of hire, given the difference in demand for workers, for example, at different time periods). But there are other dimensions of comparison that are arguably equally relevant, such as tenure, promotion rate, and social influence. The introduction of the "equal pay for equal work" argument immediately complicates even salary comparison beyond practicality, for one simple reason: who decides what work is equal? It's not possible. That's why the marketplace exists. Worse is the problem of group comparison: women should make as much as men. OK. Black women should make as much as white women. OK. Should salary then be adjusted for all parameters of race? At what level of resolution? What racial categories are "real"?

The U.S. National Institute of Health, to take a single bureaucratic example, recognizes American Indian or Alaska Native, Asian, Black, Hispanic, Native Hawaiian or other Pacific Islander, and White. But there are more than five hundred separate American Indian tribes. By what possible logic should "American Indian" therefore stand as a canonical category? Osage tribal members have a yearly average income of $30K, while Tohono O'odham's make $11K. Are they equally oppressed? What about disabilities? Disabled people should make as much as non-disabled people. OK. On the surface, that's a noble, compassionate, fair claim. But who is disabled? Is someone living with a parent with Alzheimer's disabled? If not, why not? What about someone with a lower IQ? Someone less attractive? Someone overweight? Some people clearly move through life markedly overburdened with problems that are beyond their control, but it is a rare person indeed who isn't suffering from at least one serious catastrophe at any given time— particularly if you include their family in the equation. And why shouldn't you? Here's the fundamental problem: *group identity can be fractionated right down to the level of the individual.* That sentence should be written in capital letters. Every person is unique—and not just in a trivial manner: importantly, significantly, meaningfully unique. Group membership cannot capture that variability. Period.

None of this complexity is ever discussed by the postmodern/Marxist thinkers. Instead, their ideological approach fixes a point of truth, like the North Star, and forces everything to rotate around it. The claim that all gender differences are a consequence of socialization is neither provable, nor disprovable, in some sense, because culture can be brought to bear with such force on groups or individuals that virtually any outcome is attainable, if we are willing to bear the cost. We know, for example, from studies of adopted-out identical twins,[190] that culture can produce a fifteen-point (or one standard deviation) increase in IQ (roughly the difference between the average high school student and the average state college student) at the cost of a three-standard-deviation increase in wealth.[191] What this means, approximately, is that two identical twins, separated at birth, will differ in IQ by fifteen points if the first twin is raised in a family that is poorer than 85 percent of families and the second is raised in a family richer than 95 percent of families. Something similar has recently been demonstrated with education, rather than wealth.[192] We don't know what it would cost in wealth or differential education to produce a more extreme transformation.

What such studies imply is that we could probably minimize the innate differences between boys and girls, if we were willing to exert enough pressure. This would in no way ensure that we were freeing people of either gender to make their own choices. But choice has no place in the ideological picture: if men and women act, voluntarily, to produce gender-unequal outcomes, those very choices must have been determined by cultural bias. In consequence, everyone is a brainwashed victim, wherever gender differences exist, and the rigorous critical theoretician is morally obligated to set them straight. This means that those already equity-minded Scandinavian males, who aren't much into nursing, require even more retraining. The same goes, in principle, for Scandinavian females, who aren't much into engineering.[193] What might such retraining look like? Where might its limits lie? Such things are often pushed past any reasonable limit before they are discontinued. Mao's murderous Cultural Revolution should have taught us that.

Boys into Girls

It has become a tenet of a certain kind of social constructionist theory that the world would be much improved if boys were socialized like girls. Those who put forward such theories assume, first, that aggression is a learned behaviour, and can therefore simply not be taught, and second (to take a particular example) that, "boys should be socialized the way girls have been traditionally socialized, and they should be encouraged to develop socially positive qualities such as tenderness, sensitivity to feelings, nurturance, cooperative and aesthetic appreciation." In the opinions of such thinkers, aggression will only be reduced when male adolescents and young adults "subscribe to the same standards of behavior as have been traditionally encouraged for women."[194]

There are so many things wrong with this idea that it is difficult to know where to start. First, it is not the case that aggression is merely learned. Aggression is there at the beginning. There are ancient biological circuits, so to speak, that underlie defensive and predatory aggression.[195] They are so fundamental that they still operate in what are known as decorticate cats, animals that have had the largest and most recently evolved parts of their brain—an overwhelmingly large percentage of the total structure—entirely removed. This suggests not only that aggression is innate, but that it is a consequence of activity in extremely fundamental, basic brain areas. If the brain is a tree, then aggression (along with hunger, thirst and sexual desire) is there in the very trunk.

And, in keeping with this, it appears that a subset of two-year-old boys (about 5 percent) are quite aggressive, by temperament. They take other kids' toys, kick, bite and hit. Most are nonetheless socialized effectively by the age of four.[196] This is not, however, because they have been encouraged to act like little girls. Instead, they are taught or otherwise learn in early childhood to integrate their aggressive tendencies into more sophisticated behavioural routines. Aggression underlies the drive to be outstanding, to be unstoppable, to compete, to win—to be actively virtuous, at least along one dimension. Determination is its admirable, pro-social face. Aggressive young children who don't manage to render their temperament sophisticated by the end of infancy are doomed to unpopularity, as their primordial antagonism no longer serves them socially at later ages. Rejected by their peers, they lack further socialization opportunities and tend towards outcast status. These are the individuals who remain much more inclined toward antisocial and criminal behavior when adolescent and adult. But this does not at all mean that the aggressive drive lacks either utility or value. At a minimum, it is necessary for self-protection.

Compassion as a Vice

Many of the female clients (perhaps even a majority) that I see in my clinical practice have trouble in their jobs and family lives not because they are too aggressive, but because they are not aggressive enough. Cognitive-behavioural therapists call the treatment of such people, generally characterized by the more feminine traits of agreeableness (politeness and compassion) and neuroticism (anxiety and emotional pain), "assertiveness training."[197] Insufficiently aggressive women—and men, although more rarely—do too much for others. They tend to treat those around them as if they were distressed children. They tend to be naïve. They assume that cooperation should be the basis of all social transactions, and they avoid conflict (which means they avoid confronting problems in their relationships as well as at work). They continually sacrifice for others. This may sound virtuous—and it is definitely an attitude that has certain social advantages—but it can and often does become counterproductively one-sided. Because too-agreeable people bend over backwards for other people, they do not stand up properly for themselves. Assuming that others think as they do, they expect—instead of ensuring—reciprocity for their thoughtful actions. When this does not happen, they don't speak up. They do not or cannot straightforwardly demand recognition. The dark side of their characters emerges, because of their subjugation, and they become resentful.

I teach excessively agreeable people to note the emergence of such resentment, which is a very important, although very toxic, emotion. There are only two major reasons for resentment: being taken advantage of (or allowing yourself to be taken advantage of), or whiny refusal to adopt responsibility and grow up. If you're resentful, look for the reasons. Perhaps discuss the issue with someone you trust. Are you feeling hard done by, in an immature manner? If, after some honest consideration, you don't think it's that, perhaps someone is taking advantage of you. This means that you now face a moral obligation to speak up for yourself. This might mean confronting your boss, or your husband, or your wife, or your child, or your parents. It might mean gathering some evidence, strategically, so that when you confront that person, you can give them several examples of their misbehaviour (at least three), so they can't easily weasel out of your accusations. It might mean failing to concede when they offer you their counterarguments. People rarely have more than four at hand. If you remain unmoved, they get angry, or cry, or run away. It's very useful to attend to tears in such situations. They can be used to motivate guilt on the part of the accuser due, theoretically, to having caused hurt feelings and pain. But tears are often shed in anger. A red face is a good cue. If you can push your point past the first four responses and stand fast against the consequent emotion, you will gain your target's attention—and, perhaps, their respect. This is genuine conflict, however, and it's neither pleasant nor easy.

You must also know clearly what you want out of the situation, and be prepared to clearly articulate your desire. It's a good idea to tell the person you are confronting exactly what you would like them to do instead of what they have done or currently are doing. You might think, "if they loved me, they would know what to do." That's the voice of resentment. Assume ignorance before malevolence. No one has a direct pipeline to your wants and needs—not even you. If you try to determine exactly what you want, you might find that it is more difficult than you think. The person oppressing you is likely no wiser than you, especially about you. Tell them directly what would be preferable, instead, after you have sorted it out. Make your request as small and reasonable as possible—but ensure that its fulfillment would satisfy you. In that manner, you come to the discussion with a solution, instead of just a problem.

Agreeable, compassionate, empathic, conflict-averse people (all those traits group together) let people walk on them, and they get bitter. They sacrifice themselves for others, sometimes excessively, and cannot comprehend why that is not reciprocated. Agreeable people are compliant, and this robs them of their independence. The danger associated with this can be amplified by high trait neuroticism. Agreeable people will go along with whoever makes a suggestion, instead of insisting, at least sometimes, on their own way. So, they lose their way, and become indecisive and too easily swayed. If they are, in addition, easily frightened and hurt, they have even less reason to strike out on their own, as doing so exposes them to threat and danger (at least in the short term). That's the pathway to dependent personality disorder, technically speaking.[198] It might be regarded as the polar opposite of antisocial personality disorder, the set of traits characteristic of delinquency in childhood and adolescence and criminality in adulthood. It would be lovely if the opposite of a criminal was a saint—but it's not the case. The opposite of a criminal is an Oedipal mother, which is its own type of criminal.

The Oedipal mother (and fathers can play this role too, but it's comparatively rare) says to her child, "I only live for you." She does everything for her children. She ties their shoes, and cuts up their food, and lets them crawl into bed with her and her partner far too often. That's a good and conflict-avoidant method for avoiding unwanted sexual attention, as well.

The Oedipal mother makes a pact with herself, her children, and the devil himself. The deal is this: "Above all, never leave me. In return, I will do everything for you. As you age without maturing, you will become worthless and bitter, but you will never have to take any responsibility, and everything you do that's wrong will always be someone else's fault." The children can accept or reject this—and they have some choice in the matter.

The Oedipal mother is the witch in the story of Hansel and Gretel. The two children in that fairy tale have a new step-mother. She orders her husband to abandon his children in the forest, as there is a famine and she thinks they eat too much. He obeys his wife, takes his children deep into the woods and leaves them to their fate. Wandering, starving and lonely, they come across a miracle. A house. And not just any house. A candy house. A gingerbread house. A person who had not been rendered too caring, empathic, sympathetic and cooperative might be skeptical, and ask, "Is this too good to be true?" But the children are too young, and too desperate.

Inside the house is a kind old woman, rescuer of distraught children, kind patter of heads and wiper of noses, all bosom and hips, ready to sacrifice herself to their every wish, at a moment's notice. She feeds the children anything they want, any time they want, and they never have to do anything. But provision of that kind of care makes her hungry. She puts Hansel into a cage, to fatten him up ever more efficiently. He fools her into thinking he's staying thin by offering her an old bone, when she tries to test his leg for the desired tenderness. She gets too desperate to wait, eventually, and stokes the oven, preparing to cook and eat the object of her doting. Gretel, who has apparently not been lulled into full submission, waits for a moment of carelessness, and pushes the kind old woman into the oven. The kids run away, and rejoin their father, who has thoroughly repented of his evil actions.

In a household like that, the choicest cut of child is the spirit, and it's always consumed first. Too much protection devastates the developing soul.

The witch in the Hansel and Gretel tale is the Terrible Mother, the dark half of the symbolically feminine. Deeply social as we are in our essence, we tend to view the world as a story, the characters of which are mother, father and child. The feminine, as a whole, is unknown nature outside the bounds of culture, creation and destruction: she is the protective arms of mother and the destructive element of time, the beautiful virgin-mother and the swamp-dwelling hag. This archetypal entity was confused with an objective, historical reality, back in the late 1800s, by a Swiss anthropologist named Johann Jakob Bachofen. Bachofen proposed that humanity had passed through a series of developmental stages in its history.

The first, roughly speaking (after a somewhat anarchic and chaotic beginning), was Das Mutterrecht[199]—a society where women held the dominant positions of power, respect and honour, where polyamory and promiscuity ruled, and where any certainty of paternity was absent. The second, the Dionysian, was a phase of transition, during which these original matriarchal foundations were overturned and power was taken by men. The third phase, the Apollonian, still reigns today. The patriarchy rules, and each woman belongs exclusively to one man. Bachofen's ideas became profoundly influential, in certain circles, despite the absence of any historical evidence to support them. One Marija Gimbutas, for example—an archaeologist— famously claimed in the 1980s and 1990s that a peaceful goddess-and-woman-centred culture once characterized Neolithic Europe.[200] She claimed that it was supplanted and suppressed by an invasive hierarchical warrior culture, which laid the basis for modern society. Art historian Merlin Stone made the same argument in his book *When God Was a Woman.*[201] This whole series of essentially archetypal/mythological ideas became touchstones for the theology of the women's movement and the matriarchal studies of 1970s feminism (Cynthia Eller, who wrote a book criticizing such ideas —*The Myth of Matriarchal Prehistory*—called this theology "an ennobling lie").[202]

Carl Jung had encountered Bachofen's ideas of primordial matriarchy decades earlier. Jung soon realized, however, that the developmental progression described by the earlier Swiss thinker represented a psychological rather than a historical reality. He saw in Bachofen's thought the same processes of projection of imaginative fantasy on to the external world that had led to the population of the cosmos with constellations and gods. In *The Origins and History of Consciousness*[203] and *The Great Mother*[204], Jung's collaborator Erich Neumann extended his colleague's analysis. Neumann traced the emergence of consciousness, symbolically masculine, and contrasted it with its symbolically feminine, material (mother, matrix) origins, subsuming Freud's theory of Oedipal parenting into a broader archetypal model. For Neumann, and for Jung, consciousness—always symbolically masculine, even in women—struggles upwards toward the light. Its development is painful and anxiety-provoking, as it carries with it the realization of vulnerability and death. It is constantly tempted to sink back down into dependency and unconsciousness, and to shed its existential burden. It is aided in that pathological desire by anything that opposes enlightenment, articulation, rationality, self-determination, strength and competence—by anything that shelters too much, and therefore smothers and devours. Such overprotection is Freud's Oedipal familial nightmare, which we are rapidly transforming into social policy.

The Terrible Mother is an ancient symbol. It manifests itself, for example, in the form of Tiamat, in the earliest written story we have recovered, the Mesopotamian *Enuma Elish*. Tiamat is the mother of all things, gods and men alike. She is the unknown and chaos and the nature that gives rise to all forms. But she is also the female dragon-deity who moves to destroy her own children, when they carelessly kill their father and attempt to live on the corpse that remains. The Terrible Mother is the spirit of careless unconsciousness, tempting the ever-striving spirit of awareness and enlightenment down into the protective womb-like embrace of the underworld. It's the terror young men feel towards attractive women, who are nature itself, ever ready to reject them, intimately, at the deepest possible level. Nothing inspires self-consciousness, undermines courage, and fosters feelings of nihilism and hatred more than that—except, perhaps, the too-tight embrace of too-caring mom.

The Terrible Mother appears in many fairy tales, and in many stories for adults. In the *Sleeping Beauty*, she is the Evil Queen, dark nature herself—Maleficent, in the Disney version. The royal parents of Princess Aurora fail to invite this force of the night to their baby daughter's christening. Thus, they shelter her too much from the destructive and dangerous side of reality, preferring that she grow up untroubled by such things. Their reward? At puberty, she is still unconscious. The masculine spirit, her prince, is both a man who could save her, by tearing her from her parents, and her own consciousness, trapped in a dungeon by the machinations of the dark side of femininity. When that prince escapes, and presses the Evil Queen too hard, she turns into the Dragon of Chaos itself. The symbolic masculine defeats her with truth and faith, and finds the princess, whose eyes he opens with a kiss.

It might be objected (as it was, with Disney's more recent and deeply propagandistic *Frozen*) that a woman does not need a man to rescue her. That may be true, and it may not. It may be that only the woman who wants (or has) a child needs a man to rescue her—or at least to support and aid her. In any case, it is certain that a woman needs consciousness be rescued, and, as noted above, consciousness is symbolically masculine and has been since the beginning of time (in the guise both of order and of the Logos, the mediating principle). The Prince could be a lover, but could also be a woman's own attentive wakefulness, clarity of vision, and tough-minded independence. Those are masculine traits—in actuality, as well as symbolically, as men are actually less tender-minded and agreeable than women, on average, and are less susceptible to anxiety and emotional pain. And, to say it again: (1) this is most true in those Scandinavian nations where the most steps towards gender equality have been taken—and (2) the differences are not small by the standards whereby such things are measured.

The relationship between the masculine and consciousness is also portrayed, symbolically, in the Disney movie *The Little Mermaid*. Ariel, the heroine, is quite feminine, but she also has a strong spirit of independence. For this reason, she is her father's favourite, although she also causes him the most trouble. Her father Triton is the king, representing the known, culture and order (with a hint of the oppressive rule-giver and tyrant). Because order is always opposed by chaos, Triton has an adversary, Ursula, a tentacled octopus—a serpent, a gorgon, a hydra. Thus, Ursula is in the same archetypal category as the dragon/queen Maleficent in *Sleeping Beauty* (or the jealous older queen in *Snow White*, Lady Tremaine in *Cinderella*, the Red Queen in *Alice in Wonderland*, Cruella de Vil in *101 Dalmations*, Miss Medusa in *The Rescuers* and Mother Gothel in *Tangled*).

Ariel wants to kindle a romance with Prince Eric, whom she previously rescued from a shipwreck. Ursula tricks Ariel into giving up her voice so that she can have three days as a human being. Ursula knows full well, however, that a voiceless Ariel will not be able to establish a relationship with the Prince. Without her capacity to speak—without the Logos; without the Divine Word—she will remain underwater, unconscious, forever.

When Ariel fails to form a union with Prince Eric, Ursula steals her soul, and places it in her large collection of shrivelled and warped semi-beings, well-protected by her feminine graces. When King Triton shows up to demand the return of his daughter, Ursula makes him a terrible offer: he can take Ariel's place. Of course, the elimination of the Wise King (who represents, to say it again, the benevolent side of the patriarchy) has been Ursula's nefarious plan all along. Ariel is released, but Triton is now reduced to a pathetic shadow of his former self. More importantly, Ursula now has Triton's magic trident, the source of his godlike power.

Fortunately for everyone concerned (except Ursula), Prince Eric returns, distracting the evil queen of the underworld with a harpoon. This opens an opportunity for Ariel to attack Ursula, who grows, in response, to monstrous proportions—in the same manner as Maleficent, *Sleeping Beauty*'s evil queen. Ursula creates a huge storm, and raises a whole navy of sunken ships from the ocean floor. As she prepares to kill Ariel, Eric commandeers a wrecked ship, and rams her with its broken bowsprit. Triton and the other captured souls are released. The rejuvenated Triton then transforms his daughter into a human being, so she can remain with Eric. For a woman to become complete, such stories claim, she must form a relationship with masculine consciousness and stand up to the terrible world (which sometimes manifests itself, primarily, in the form of her too-present mother). An actual man can help her do that, to some degree, but it is better for everyone concerned when no one is too dependent.

One day, when I was a kid, I was out playing softball with some friends. The teams were a mixture of boys and girls. We were all old enough so that the boys and girls were starting to be interested in one another in an unfamiliar way. Status was becoming more relevant and important. My friend

Jake and I were about to come to blows, pushing each other around near the pitching mound, when my mom walked by. She was a fair distance away, about thirty yards, but I could immediately see by the change in her body language that she knew what was going on. Of course, the other kids saw her as well. She walked right by. I knew that hurt her. Part of her was worried that I would come home with a bloody nose and a black eye. It would have been easy enough for her just to yell, "Hey, you kids, quit that!" or even to come over and interfere. But she didn't. A few years later, when I was having teenage trouble with my dad, my mom said, "If it was too good at home, you'd never leave."

My mom is a tender-hearted person. She's empathetic, and cooperative, and agreeable. Sometimes she lets people push her around. When she went back to work after being at home with her young kids, she found it challenging to stand up to the men. Sometimes that made her resentful—something she also feels, sometimes, in relationship to my father, who is strongly inclined to do what he wants, when he wants to. Despite all that, she's no Oedipal mother. She fostered the independence of her children, even though doing so was often hard on her. She did the right thing, even though it caused her emotional distress.

Toughen Up, You Weasel

I spent one youthful summer on the prairie of central Saskatchewan working on a railway line crew. Every man in that all-male group was tested by the others during the first two weeks or so of their hiring. Many of the other workers were Northern Cree Indians, quiet guys for the most part, easygoing, until they drank too much, and the chips on their shoulders started to show. They had been in and out of jail, as had most of their relatives. They didn't attach much shame to that, considering it just another part of the white man's system. It was also warm in jail in the winter, and the food was regular and plentiful. I lent one of the Cree guys fifty bucks at one point. Instead of paying me back, he offered me a pair of bookends, cut from some of the original rail laid across western Canada, which I still own. That was better than the fifty bucks.

When a new guy first showed up, the other workers would inevitably provide him with an insulting nickname. They called me Howdy-Doody, after I was accepted as a crew member (something I am still slightly embarrassed to admit). When I asked the originator why he chose that moniker, he said, wittily and absurdly, "Because you look nothing like him." Working men are often extremely funny, in a caustic, biting, insulting manner (as discussed in Rule 9). They are always harassing each other, partly for amusement, partly to score points in the eternal dominance battle between them, but also partly to see what the other guy will do if he is subjected to social stress. It's part of the process of character evaluation, as well as camaraderie. When it works well (when everybody gets, and gives as good as they get, and can give and take) it's a big part of what allows men who work for a living to tolerate or even enjoy laying pipe and working on oil rigs and lumberjacking and working in restaurant kitchens and all the other hot, dirty, physically demanding and dangerous work that is still done almost totally by men.

Not too long after I started on the rail crew, my name was changed to Howdy. This was a great improvement, as it had a good Western connotation, and was not obviously linked to that stupid puppet. The next man hired was not so fortunate. He carried a fancy lunchbucket, which was a mistake, as brown paper bags were the proper, non-pretentious convention. It was a little too nice and too new. It looked like maybe his mother had bought it (and packed it) for him. Thus, it became his name. Lunchbucket was not a good-humored guy. He bitched about everything, and had a bad attitude. Everything was someone else's fault. He was touchy, and none too quick on the draw.

Lunchbucket couldn't accept his name, or settle into his job. He adopted an attitude of condescending irritation when addressed, and reacted to the work in the same manner. He was not fun to be around, and he couldn't take a joke. That's fatal, on a work crew. After about three days of carrying on with his ill-humour and general air of hard-done-by superiority, Lunchbucket started to experience harassment extending well beyond his nickname. He would be peevishly working away on the line, surrounded by about seventy men, spread out over a quarter mile. Suddenly a pebble would appear out of nowhere, flying through the air, aimed at his hardhat. A direct hit would produce a thunking sound, deeply satisfying to all the quietly attending onlookers. Even this failed to improve his humour. So, the pebbles got larger. Lunchbucket would involve himself in something and forget to pay attention.

Then, "thunk!"—a well-aimed stone would nail him on the noggin, producing a burst of irritated and ineffectual fury. Quiet amusement would ripple down the rail line. After a few days of this, no wiser, and carrying a few bruises, Lunchbucket vanished.

Men enforce a code of behaviour on each other, when working together. Do your work. Pull your weight. Stay awake and pay attention. Don't whine or be touchy. Stand up for your friends. Don't suck up and don't snitch. Don't be a slave to stupid rules. Don't, in the immortal words of Arnold Schwarzenegger, be a girlie man. Don't be dependent. At all. Ever. Period. The harassment that is part of acceptance on a working crew is a test: are you tough, entertaining, competent and reliable? If not, go away. Simple as that. We don't need to feel sorry for you. We don't want to put up with your narcissism, and we don't want to do your work.

There was a famous advertisement in the form of a comic strip issued a few decades ago by the bodybuilder Charles Atlas. It was titled "The Insult that Made a Man out of Mac" and could be found in almost every comic book, most of which were read by boys. Mac, the protagonist, is sitting on a beach blanket with an attractive young woman. A bully runs by, and kicks sand in both their faces. Mac objects. The much larger man grabs him by the arm and says, "Listen here. I'd smash your face .... Only you're so skinny you might dry up and blow away." The bully departs. Mac says to the girl, "The big bully! I'll get even some day." She adopts a provocative pose, and says, "Oh, don't let it bother you, little boy." Mac goes home, considers his pathetic physique, and buys the Atlas program. Soon, he has a new body. The next time he goes to the beach, he punches the bully in the nose. The now-admiring girl clings to his arm. "Oh, Mac!" she says. "You're a real man after all."

That ad is famous for a reason. It summarizes human sexual psychology in seven straightforward panels. The too-weak young man is embarrassed and self-conscious, as he should be. What good is he? He gets put down by other men and, worse, by desirable women. Instead of drowning in resentment, and skulking off to his basement to play video games in his underwear, covered with Cheetos dust, he presents himself with what Alfred Adler, Freud's most practical colleague, called a "compensatory fantasy."[205] The goal of such a fantasy is not so much wish-fulfillment, as illumination of a genuine path forward. Mac takes serious note of his scarecrow-like build and decides that he should develop a stronger body. More importantly, he puts his plan into action. He identifies with the part of himself that could transcend his current state, and becomes the hero of his own adventure. He goes back to the beach, and punches the bully in the nose. Mac wins. So does his eventual girlfriend. So does everybody else.

It is to women's clear advantage that men do not happily put up with dependency among themselves. Part of the reason that so many a working-class woman does not marry, now, as we have alluded to, is because she does not want to look after a man, struggling for employment, as well as her children. And fair enough. A woman should look after her children—although that is not all she should do. And a man should look after a woman and children—although that is not all he should do. But a woman should not look after a man, because she must look after children, and a man should not be a child. This means that he must not be dependent. This is one of the reasons that men have little patience for dependent men. And let us not forget: wicked women may produce dependent sons, may support and even marry dependent men, but awake and conscious women want an awake and conscious partner.

If is for this reason that Nelson Muntz of *The Simpsons* is so necessary to the small social group that surrounds Homer's antihero son, Bart. Without Nelson, King of the Bullies, the school would soon be overrun by resentful, touchy Milhouses, narcissistic, intellectual Martin Princes, soft, chocolate-gorging German children, and infantile Ralph Wiggums. Muntz is a corrective, a tough, self-sufficient kid who uses his own capacity for contempt to decide what line of immature and pathetic behaviour simply cannot be crossed. Part of the genius of *The Simpsons* is its writers' refusal to simply write Nelson off as an irredeemable bully. Abandoned by his worthless father, neglected, thankfully, by his thoughtless slut of a mother, Nelson does pretty well, everything considered. He's even of romantic interest to the thoroughly progressive Lisa, much to her dismay and confusion (for much the same reasons that *Fifty Shades of Grey* became a worldwide phenomenon).

When softness and harmlessness become the only consciously acceptable virtues, then hardness and dominance will start to exert an unconscious fascination. Partly what this means for the future is that if men are pushed too hard to feminize, they will become more and more interested in harsh, fascist political ideology. *Fight Club*, perhaps the most fascist popular film made in recent years by Hollywood, with the possible exception of the Iron Man series, provides a perfect example of such inevitable attraction. The populist groundswell of support for Donald Trump in the US is part of the same process, as is (in far more sinister form) the recent rise of far-right political parties even in such moderate and liberal places as Holland, Sweden and Norway.

Men have to toughen up. Men demand it, and women want it, even though they may not approve of the harsh and contemptuous attitude that is part and parcel of the socially demanding process that fosters and then enforces that toughness. Some women don't like losing their baby boys, so they keep them forever. Some women don't like men, and would rather have a submissive mate, even if he is useless. This also provides them with plenty to feel sorry for themselves about, as well. The pleasures of such self-pity should not be underestimated.

Men toughen up by pushing themselves, and by pushing each other. When I was a teenager, the boys were much more likely to get into car accidents than the girls (as they still are). This was because they were out spinning donuts at night in icy parking lots. They were drag racing and driving their cars over the roadless hills extending from the nearby river up to the level land hundreds of feet higher. They were more likely to fight physically, and to skip class, and to tell the teachers off, and to quit school because they were tired of raising their hands for permission to go to the bathroom when they were big and strong enough to work on the oil rigs. They were more likely to race their motorbikes on frozen lakes in the winter. Like the skateboarders, and crane climbers, and free runners, they were doing dangerous things, trying to make themselves useful. When this process goes too far, boys (and men) drift into the antisocial behavior which is far more prevalent in males than in females.[206] That does not mean that every manifestation of daring and courage is criminal.

When the boys were spinning donuts, they were also testing the limits of their cars, their ability as drivers, and their capacity for control, in an out-of-control situation. When they told off the teachers, they were pushing against authority, to see if there was any real authority there—the kind that could be relied on, in principle, in a crisis. When they quit school, they went to work as rig roughnecks when it was forty bloody degrees below zero. It wasn't weakness that propelled so many out of the classroom, where a better future arguably awaited. It was strength.

If they're healthy, women don't want boys. They want men. They want someone to contend with; someone to grapple with. If they're tough, they want someone tougher. If they're smart, they want someone smarter. They desire someone who brings to the table something they can't already provide. This often makes it hard for tough, smart, attractive women to find mates: there just aren't that many men around who can outclass them enough to be considered desirable (who are higher, as one research publication put it, in "income, education, self-confidence, intelligence, dominance and social position").[207] The spirit that interferes when boys are trying to become men is, therefore, no more friend to woman than it is to man. It will object, just as vociferously and self-righteously ("you can't do it, it's too dangerous") when little girls try to stand on their own two feet. It negates consciousness. It's antihuman, desirous of failure, jealous, resentful and destructive. No one truly on the side of humanity would ally him or herself with such a thing. No one aiming at moving up would allow him or herself to become possessed by such a thing. And if you think tough men are dangerous, wait until you see what weak men are capable of.

Leave children alone when they are skateboarding.

PET A CAT WHEN YOU ENCOUNTER ONE ON THE STREET

DOGS ARE OK TOO

I am going to start this chapter by stating directly that I own a dog, an American Eskimo, one of the many variants of the basic spitz type. They were known as German spitzes until the First World War made it verboten to admit that anything good could come from Germany. American Eskimos are among the most beautiful of dogs, with a pointed, classic wolf face, upright ears, a long thick coat, and a curly tail. They are also very intelligent. Our dog, whose name is Sikko (which means "ice" in an Inuit language, according to my daughter, who named him), learns tricks very rapidly, and can do so even now that he's old. I taught him a new stunt, recently, when he turned thirteen. He already knew how to shake a paw, and to balance a treat on his nose. I taught him to do both at the same time. However, it's not at all clear he enjoys it.

We bought Sikko for my daughter, Mikhaila, when she was about ten years old. He was an unbearably cute pup. Small nose and ears, rounded face, big eyes, awkward movements—these features automatically elicit caretaking behaviour from humans, male and female alike.[208] This was certainly the case with Mikhaila, who was also occupied with the care of bearded dragons, gekkoes, ball pythons, chameleons, iguanas and a twenty-pound, thirty-two-inch-long Flemish Giant rabbit named George, who nibbled on everything in the house and frequently escaped (to the great consternation of those who then spied his improbably large form in their tiny mid-city gardens). She had all these animals because she was allergic to the more typical pets— excepting Sikko, who had the additional advantage of being hypo-allergenic.

Sikko garnered fifty nicknames (we counted) which varied broadly in their emotional tone, and reflected both the affection in which he was held and our occasional frustration with his beastly habits. Scumdog was probably my favorite, but I also held Rathound, Furball and Suck-dog in rather high esteem. The kids used Sneak and Squeak (sometimes with an appended o) most frequently, but accompanied it with Snooky, Ugdog, and Snorfalopogus (horrible though it is to admit). Snorbs is Mikhaila's current moniker of choice. She uses it to greet him after a prolonged absence. For full effect, it must be uttered in a high-pitched and surprised voice.

Sikko also happens to have his own Instagram hashtag: #JudgementalSikko.

I am describing my dog instead of writing directly about cats because I don't wish to run afoul of a phenomenon known as "minimal group identification," discovered by the social psychologist Henri Tajfel.[209] Tajfel brought his research subjects into his lab and sat them down in front of a screen, onto which he flashed a number of dots. The subjects were asked to estimate their quantity. Then he categorized his subjects as overestimators vs underestimators, as well as accurate vs inaccurate, and put them into groups corresponding to their performance. Then he asked them to divide money among the members of all the groups.

Tajfel found that his subjects displayed a marked preference for their own group members, rejecting an egalitarian distribution strategy and disproportionately rewarding those with whom they now identified. Other researchers have assigned people to different groups using ever more arbitrary strategies, such as flipping a coin. It didn't matter, even when the subjects were informed of the way the groups were composed. People still favoured the co-members of their personal group.

Tajfel's studies demonstrated two things: first, *that people are social*; second, *that people are antisocial*. People are social because they like the members of their own group. People are antisocial because they don't like the members of other groups. Exactly why this is so has been the subject of continual debate. I think it might be a solution to a complex problem of optimization. Such problems arise, for example, when two or more factors are important, but none cannot be maximized without diminishing the others. A problem of this sort emerges, for example, because of the antipathy between cooperation and competition, both of which are socially and psychologically desirable. Cooperation is for safety, security and companionship. Competition is for personal growth and status. However, if a given group is too small, it has no power or prestige, and cannot fend off other groups. In consequence, being one of its members is not that useful. If the group is too large, however, the probability of climbing near or to the top declines. So, it becomes too hard to get ahead. Perhaps people identify with groups at the flip of a coin because they deeply want to organize themselves, protect themselves, and still have some reasonable probability of climbing the dominance hierarchy. Then they favour their own group, because favouring it helps it thrive—and climbing something that is failing is not a useful strategy.

In any case, it is because of Tajfel's minimal-conditions discovery that I began this cat-related chapter with a description of my dog. Otherwise, the mere mention of a cat in the title would be enough to turn many dog people against me, just because I didn't include canines in the group of entities that should be petted. Since I also like dogs, there is no reason for me to suffer such a fate. So, if you like to pet dogs when you meet them on the street, don't feel obliged to hate me. Rest assured, instead, that this is also an activity of which I approve. I would also like to apologize to all the cat people who now feel slighted, because they were hoping for a cat story but had to read all this dog-related material. Perhaps they might be satisfied by some assurance that cats do illustrate the point I want to make better, and that I will eventually discuss them. First, however, to other things.

Suffering and the Limitations of Being

The idea that life is suffering is a tenet, in one form or another, of every major religious doctrine, as we have already discussed. Buddhists state it directly. Christians illustrate it with the cross. Jews commemorate the suffering endured over centuries. Such reasoning universally characterizes the great creeds, because human beings are intrinsically fragile. We can be damaged, even broken, emotionally and physically, and we are all subject to the depredations of aging and loss. This is a dismal set of facts, and it is reasonable to wonder how we can expect to thrive and be happy (or even to want to exist, sometimes) under such conditions.

I was speaking recently with a client whose husband had been engaging in a successful battle with cancer for an agonizing period of five years. They had both held up remarkably and courageously over this period. However, he fell prey to the tendency of that dread condition to metastasize and, in consequence, had been given very little time to live. It is perhaps hardest to hear terrible news like this when you are still in the fragile post-recovery state that occurs after dealing successfully with previous bad news. Tragedy at such a time seems particularly unfair. It is the sort of thing that can make you distrust even hope itself. It's frequently sufficient to cause genuine trauma. My client and I discussed a number of issues, some philosophical and abstract, some more concrete. I shared with her some of the thoughts that I had developed about the whys and wherefores of human vulnerability.

When my son, Julian, was about three, he was particularly cute. He's twenty years older than that now, but still quite cute (a compliment I'm sure he'll particularly enjoy reading). Because of him, I thought a lot about the fragility of small children. A three-year-old is easily damaged. Dogs can bite him. Cars can hit him. Mean kids can push him over. He can get sick (and sometimes did). Julian was prone to high fevers and the delirium they sometimes produce. Sometimes I had to take him into the shower with me and cool him off when he was hallucinating, or even fighting with me, in his feverish state. There are few things that make it harder to accept the fundamental limitations of human existence than a sick child.

Mikhaila, a year and a few months older than Julian, also had her problems. When she was two, I would lift her up on my shoulders and carry her around. Kids enjoy that. Afterwards, however, when I put her feet back on the ground, she would sit down and cry. So, I stopped doing it. That seemed to be the end of the problem—with a seemingly minor exception. My wife, Tammy, told me that something was wrong with Mikhaila's gait. I couldn't see it. Tammy thought it might be related to her reaction to being carried on my shoulders.

Mikhaila was a sunny child and very easy to get along with. One day when she was about fourteen months old I took her along with Tammy and her grandparents to Cape Cod, when we lived in Boston. When we got there, Tammy and her mom and dad walked ahead, and left me with Mikhaila in the car. We were in the front seat. She was lying there in the sun, babbling away. I leaned over to hear what she was saying.

"Happy, happy, happy, happy, happy."

That's what she was like.

When she turned six, however, she started to get mopey. It was hard to get her out of bed in the morning. She put on her clothes very slowly. When we walked somewhere, she lagged behind. She complained that her feet hurt and that her shoes didn't fit. We bought her ten different pairs, but it didn't help. She went to school, and held her head up, and behaved properly. But when she came home, and saw her Mom, she would break into tears.

We had recently moved from Boston to Toronto, and attributed these changes to the stress of the move. But it didn't get better. Mikhaila began to walk up and down stairs one step at a time. She began to move like someone much older. She complained if you held her hand. (One time, much later, she asked me, "Dad, when you played 'this little piggy,' with me when I was little, was it supposed to hurt?" Things you learn too late …).

A physician at our local medical clinic told us, "Sometimes children have growing pains. They're normal. But you could think about taking her to see a physiotherapist." So, we did. The physiotherapist tried to rotate Mikhaila's heel. It didn't move. That was not good. The physio told us, "Your daughter has juvenile rheumatoid arthritis." This was not what we wanted to hear. We did not like that physiotherapist. We went back to the medical clinic. Another physician there told us to take Mikhaila to the Hospital for Sick Children. The doctor said, "Take her to the emergency room. That way, you will be able to see a rheumatologist quickly." Mikhaila had arthritis, all right. The physio, bearer of unwelcome news, was correct. Thirty-seven affected joints. Severe polyarticular juvenile idiopathic arthritis (JIA). Cause? Unknown. Prognosis? Multiple early joint replacements.

What sort of God would make a world where such a thing could happen, at all?—much less to an innocent and happy little girl? It's a question of absolutely fundamental import, for believer and non-believer alike. It's an issue addressed (as are so many difficult matters) in *The Brothers Karamazov*, the great novel by Dostoevsky we began to discuss in Rule 7. Dostoevsky expresses his doubts about the propriety of Being through the character of Ivan who, if you remember, is the articulate, handsome, sophisticated brother (and greatest adversary) of the monastic novitiate Alyosha. "It's not God I don't accept. Understand this," says Ivan. "I do not accept the world that He created, this world of God's, and cannot agree with it."

Ivan tells Alyosha a story about a small girl whose parents punished her by locking her in a freezing outhouse overnight (a story Dostoevsky culled from a newspaper of the time). "Can you just see those two snoozing away while their daughter was crying all night?" says Ivan. "And imagine this little child: unable to understand what was happening to her, beating her frozen little chest and crying meek little tears, begging 'gentle Jesus' to get her out of that horrible place! … Alyosha: if you were somehow promised that the world could finally have complete and total peace—but only on the condition that you tortured one little child to death—say, that girl who was freezing in the outhouse … would you do it?" Alyosha demurs. "No, I would not," he says, softly.[210] He would not do what God seems to freely allow.

I had realized something relevant to this, years before, about three-year-old Julian (remember him? :)). I thought, "I love my son. He's three, and cute and little and comical. But I am also afraid for him, because he could be hurt. If I had the power to change that, what might I do?" I thought, "He could be twenty feet tall instead of forty inches. Nobody could push him over then. He could be made of titanium, instead of flesh and bone. Then, if some brat bounced a toy truck off his noggin, he wouldn't care. He could have a computer-enhanced brain. And even if he was damaged, somehow, his parts could be immediately replaced. Problem solved!" But no—not problem solved—and not just because such things are currently impossible. Artificially fortifying Julian would have been the same as destroying him. Instead of his little three-year-old self, he would be a cold, steel-hard robot. That wouldn't be Julian. It would be a monster. I came to realize through such thoughts that what can be truly loved about a person is inseparable from their limitations. Julian wouldn't have been little and cute and lovable if he wasn't also prone to illness, and loss, and pain, and anxiety. Since I loved him a lot, I decided that he was all right the way he was, despite his fragility.

It's been harder with my daughter. As her disease progressed, I began to piggy-back her around (not on my shoulders) when we went for walks. She started taking oral naproxen and methotrexate, the latter a powerful chemotherapy agent. She had a number of cortisol injections (wrists, shoulders, ankles, elbows, knees, hips, fingers, toes and tendons), all under general anaesthetic. This helped temporarily, but her decline continued. One day Tammy took Mikhaila to the zoo. She pushed her around in a wheelchair.

That was not a good day.

Her rheumatologist suggested prednisone, a corticosteroid, long used to fight inflammation. But prednisone has many side effects, not the least of which is severe facial swelling. It wasn't clear that this was better than the arthritis, not for a little girl. Fortunately, if that is the right word, the rheumatologist told us of a new drug. It had been used previously, but only on adults. So Mikhaila became the first Canadian child to receive etanercept, a "biological" specifically designed for autoimmune diseases. Tammy accidentally administered ten times the recommended dose the first few injections. Poof! Mikhaila was fixed. A few weeks after the trip to the zoo, she was zipping around, playing little league soccer. Tammy spent all summer just watching her run.

We wanted Mikhaila to control as much of her life as she could. She had always been strongly motivated by money. One day we found her outside, surrounded by the books of her early childhood, selling them to passersby. I sat her down one evening and told her that I would give her fifty dollars if she could do the injection herself. She was eight. She struggled for thirty-five minutes, holding the needle close to her thigh. Then she did it. Next time I paid her twenty dollars, but only gave her ten minutes. Then it was ten dollars, and five minutes. We stayed at ten for quite a while. It was a bargain.

After a few years, Mikhaila became completely symptom-free. The rheumatologist suggested that we start weaning her off her medications. Some children grow out of JIA when they hit puberty. No one knows why. She began to take methotrexate in pill form, instead of injecting it. Things were good for four years. Then, one day, her elbow started to ache. We took her back to the hospital. "You only have one actively arthritic joint," said the rheumatologist's assistant. It wasn't "only." Two isn't much more than one, but one is a lot more than zero. One meant she hadn't grown out of her arthritis, despite the hiatus. The news demolished her for a month, but she was still in dance class and playing ball games with her friends on the street in front of our house.

The rheumatologist had some more unpleasant things to say the next September, when Mikhaila started grade eleven. An MRI revealed joint deterioration at the hip. She told Mikhaila, "Your hip will have to be replaced before you turn thirty." Perhaps the damage had been done, before the etanercept worked its miracle? We didn't know. It was ominous news. One day, a few weeks after, Mikhaila was playing ball hockey in her high school gym. Her hip locked up. She had to hobble off the court. It started to hurt more and more. The rheumatologist said, "Some of your femur appears to be dead. You don't need a hip replacement when you're thirty. You need one now."

As I sat with my client—as she discussed her husband's advancing illness —we discussed the fragility of life, the catastrophe of existence, and the sense of nihilism evoked by the spectre of death. I started with my thoughts about my son. She had asked, like everyone in her situation, "Why my husband? Why me? Why this?" My realization of the tight interlinking between vulnerability and Being was the best answer I had for her. I told her an old Jewish story, which I believe is part of the commentary on the Torah. It begins with a question, structured like a Zen koan. *Imagine a Being who is omniscient, omnipresent, and omnipotent. What does such a Being lack?*[211] The answer? *Limitation.*

If you are already everything, everywhere, always, there is nowhere to go and nothing to be. Everything that could be already is, and everything that could happen already has. And it is for this reason, so the story goes, that God created man. No limitation, no story. No story, no Being. That idea has helped me deal with the terrible fragility of Being. It helped my client, too. I don't want to overstate the significance of this. I don't want to claim that this somehow makes it all OK. She still faced the cancer afflicting her husband, just as I still faced my daughter's terrible illness. But there's something to be said for recognizing that existence and limitation are inextricably linked.

> *Though thirty spokes may form the wheel,*
> *it is the hole within the hub*
> *which gives the wheel utility.*
> *It is not the clay the potter throws,*
> *which gives the pot its usefulness,*
> *but the space within the shape,*
> *from which the pot is made.*
> *Without a door, the room cannot be entered,*
> *and without its windows it is dark*
>
> *Such is the utility of non-existence.*[212]

A realization of this sort emerged more recently, in the pop culture world, during the evolution of the DC Comics cultural icon Superman. Superman was created in 1938 by Jerry Siegel and Joe Shuster. In the beginning, he could move cars, trains and even ships. He could run faster than a locomotive. He could "leap over tall buildings in a single bound." As he developed over the next four decades, however, Superman's power began to expand. By the late sixties, he could fly faster than light. He had super-hearing and X-ray vision. He could blast heat-rays from his eyes. He could freeze objects and generate hurricanes with his breath. He could move entire planets. Nuclear blasts didn't faze him. And, if he did get hurt, somehow, he would immediately heal. Superman became invulnerable.

Then a strange thing happened. He got boring. The more amazing his abilities became, the harder it was to think up interesting things for him to do. DC first overcame this problem in the 1940s. Superman became vulnerable to the radiation produced by kryptonite, a material remnant of his shattered home planet. Eventually, more than two dozen variants emerged. Green kryptonite weakened Superman. In sufficient dosage, it could even kill him. Red caused him to behave strangely. Red-green caused him to mutate (he once grew a third eye in the back of his head).

Other techniques were necessary to keep Superman's story compelling. In 1976, he was scheduled to battle Spiderman. It was the first superhero cross-over between Stan Lee's upstart Marvel Comics, with its less idealized characters, and DC, the owner of Superman and Batman. But Marvel had to augment Spiderman's powers for the battle to remain plausible. That broke the rules of the game. Spiderman is Spiderman because he has the powers of a spider. If he is suddenly granted any old power, he's not Spiderman. The plot falls apart.

By the 1980s, Superman was suffering from terminal deus ex machina—a Latin term meaning "god from a machine." The term described the rescue of the imperilled hero in ancient Greek and Romans plays by the sudden and miraculous appearance of an all-powerful god. In badly written stories, to this very day, a character in trouble can be saved or a failing plot redeemed by a bit of implausible magic or other chicanery not in keeping with the reader's reasonable expectations. Sometimes Marvel Comics, for example, saves a failing story in exactly this manner. Lifeguard, for example, is an X-Man character who can develop whatever power is necessary to save a life. He's very handy to have around. Other examples abound in popular culture. At the end of Stephen King's *The Stand*, for example (spoiler alert), God Himself destroys the novel's evil characters. The entire ninth season (1985–86) of the primetime soap *Dallas* was later revealed as a dream. Fans object to such things, and rightly so. They've been ripped off. People following a story are willing to suspend disbelief as long as the limitations making the story possible are coherent and consistent. Writers, for their part, agree to abide by their initial decisions. When writers cheat, fans get annoyed. They want to toss the book in the fireplace, and throw a brick through the TV.

And that became Superman's problem: he developed powers so extreme that he could "deus" himself out of anything, at any time. In consequence, in the 1980s, the franchise nearly died. Artist-writer John Byrne successfully rebooted it, rewriting Superman, retaining his biography, but depriving him of many of his new powers. He could no longer lift planets, or shrug off an H-bomb. He also became dependent on the sun for his power, like a reverse vampire. He gained some reasonable limitations. A superhero who can do anything turns out to be no hero at all. He's nothing specific, so he's nothing. He has nothing to strive against, so he can't be admirable. *Being of any reasonable sort appears to require limitation.* Perhaps this is because Being requires Becoming, perhaps, as well as mere static existence—and to become is to become something more, or at least something different. That is only possible for something limited.

Fair enough.

But what about the suffering caused by such limits? Perhaps the limits required by Being are so extreme that the whole project should just be scrapped. Dostoevsky expresses this idea very clearly in the voice of the protagonist of *Notes from Underground*: "So you see, you can say anything about world history—anything and everything that the most morbid imagination can think up. Except one thing, that is. It cannot be said that world history is reasonable. The word sticks in one's throat."[213] Goethe's Mephistopheles, the adversary of Being, announces his opposition explicitly to God's creation in *Faust*, as we have seen. Years later, Goethe wrote *Faust, Part II*. He has the Devil repeat his credo, in a slightly different form, just to hammer home the point:[214]

> *Gone, to sheer Nothing, past with null made one!*
> *What matters our creative endless toil,*
> *When, at a snatch, oblivion ends the coil?*
> *"It is by-gone"—How shall this riddle run?*
> *As good as if things never had begun,*
> *Yet circle back, existence to possess:*
> *I'd rather have Eternal Emptiness.*

Anyone can understand such words, when a dream collapses, a marriage ends, or a family member is struck down by a devastating disease. How can reality be structured so unbearably? How can this be?

Perhaps, as the Columbine boys suggested (see Rule 6), it would be better not to be at all. Perhaps it would be even better if there was no Being at all. But people who come to the former conclusion are flirting with suicide, and those who come to the latter with something worse, something truly monstrous. They're consorting with the idea of the destruction of everything. They are toying with genocide—and worse. Even the darkest regions have still darker corners. And what is truly horrifying is that such conclusions are understandable, maybe even inevitable—although not inevitably acted upon. What is a reasonable person to think when faced, for example, with a suffering child? Is it not precisely the reasonable person, the compassionate person, who would find such thoughts occupying his mind? How could a good God allow such a world as this to exist?

Logical they might be. Understandable, they might be. But there is a terrible catch to such conclusions. Acts undertaken in keeping with them (if not the thoughts themselves) inevitably serve to make a bad situation even worse. Hating life, despising life—even for the genuine pain that life inflicts —merely serves to make life itself worse, unbearably worse. There is no genuine protest in that. There is no goodness in that, only the desire to produce suffering, for the sake of suffering. That is the very essence of evil. People who come to that kind of thinking are one step from total mayhem. Sometimes they merely lack the tools. Sometimes, like Stalin, they have their finger on the nuclear button.

But is there any coherent alternative, given the self-evident horrors of existence? Can Being itself, with its malarial mosquitoes, child soldiers and degenerative neurological diseases, truly be justified? I'm not sure I could have formulated a proper answer to such a question in the nineteenth century, before the totalitarian horrors of the twentieth were monstrously perpetrated on millions of people. I don't know that it's possible to understand why such doubts are morally impermissible without the fact of the Holocaust and the Stalinist purges and Mao's catastrophic Great Leap Forward.[215] And I also don't think it is possible to answer the question by *thinking*. Thinking leads inexorably to the abyss. It did not work for Tolstoy. It might not even have worked for Nietzsche, who arguably thought more clearly about such things than anyone in history. But if it is not thinking that can be relied upon in the direst of situations, what is left? Thought, after all, is the highest of human achievements, is it not?

Perhaps not.

Something supersedes thinking, despite its truly awesome power. When existence reveals itself as existentially intolerable, thinking collapses in on itself. In such situations—in the depths—it's *noticing*, not thinking, that does the trick. Perhaps you might start by noticing this: when you love someone, *it's not despite their limitations. It's because of their limitations*. Of course, it's complicated. You don't have to be in love with every shortcoming, and merely accept. You shouldn't stop trying to make life better, or let suffering just be. But there appear to be limits on the path to improvement beyond which we might not want to go, lest we sacrifice our humanity itself. Of course, it's one thing to say, "Being requires limitation," and then to go about happily, when the sun is shining and your father is free of Alzheimer's disease and your kids are healthy and your marriage happy. But when things go wrong?

Disintegration and Pain

Mikhaila stayed awake many nights when she was in pain. When her grandfather came to visit, he gave her a few of his Tylenol 3s, which contain codeine. Then she could sleep. But not for long. Our rheumatologist, instrumental in producing Mikhaila's remission, hit the limit of her courage when dealing with our child's pain. She had once prescribed opiates to a young girl, who became addicted. She swore never to do so again. She said, "Have you tried ibuprofen?" Mikhaila learned then that doctors don't know everything. Ibuprofen for her was a crumb of bread for a starving man.

We talked to a new doctor. He listened carefully. Then he helped Mikhaila. First, he prescribed T3s, the same medication her grandfather had briefly shared. This was brave. Physicians face a lot of pressure to avoid the prescription of opiates—not least to children. But opiates *work*. Soon, however, the Tylenol was insufficient. She started taking oxycontin, an opioid known pejoratively as hillbilly heroin. This controlled her pain, but produced other problems. Tammy took Mikhaila out for lunch a week after the prescription started. She could have been drunk. Her speech was slurred. Her head nodded. This was not good.

My sister-in-law is a palliative care nurse. She thought we could add Ritalin, an amphetamine often used for hyperactive kids, to the oxycontin. The Ritalin restored Mikhaila's alertness and had some pain-suppressing qualities of its own (this is a very a good thing to know if you are ever faced with someone's intractable suffering). But her pain became increasingly excruciating. She started to fall. Then her hip seized up on her again, this time in the subway on a day when the escalator was not working. Her boyfriend carried her up the stairs. She took a cab home. The subway was no longer a reliable form of transportation. That March we bought Mikhaila a 50cc motor scooter. It was dangerous to let her ride it. It was also dangerous for her to lack all freedom. We chose the former danger. She passed her learner's exam, which allowed her to pilot the vehicle during the day. She was given a few months to progress towards her permanent licence.

In May her hip was replaced. The surgeon was even able to adjust for a pre-existent half centimetre difference in leg length. The bone hadn't died, either. That was only a shadow on the x-ray. Her aunt and her grandparents came to see her. We had some better days. Immediately after the surgery, however, Mikhaila was placed in an adult rehabilitation centre. She was the youngest person in the place, by about sixty years. Her aged roommate, very neurotic, wouldn't allow the lights to be off, even at night. The old woman couldn't make it to the toilet and had to use a bedpan. She couldn't stand to have the door to her room closed. But it was right beside the nurses' station, with its continual alarm bells and loud conversations. There was no sleeping there, where sleeping was required. No visitors were allowed after 7 p.m. The physio—the very reason for her placement—was on vacation. The only person who helped her was the janitor, who volunteered to move her to a multi-bed ward when she told the on-duty nurse that she couldn't sleep. This was the same nurse who had laughed when she'd found out which room Mikhaila had been assigned to.

She was supposed to be there for six weeks. She was there three days. When the vacationing physio returned, Mikhaila climbed the rehab-centre stairs and immediately mastered her additional required exercises. While she was doing that, we outfitted our home with the necessary handrails. Then we took her home. All that pain and surgery—she handled that fine. The appalling rehab centre? That produced post-traumatic stress symptoms.

Mikhaila enrolled in a full-fledged motorcycle course in June, so she could continue legally using her scooter. We were all terrified by this necessity. What if she fell? What if she had an accident? On the first day, Mikhaila trained on a real motorcycle. It was heavy. She dropped it several times. She saw another beginning rider tumble and roll across the parking lot where the course was held. On the morning of the second day of the course, she was afraid to return. She didn't want to leave her bed. We talked for a good while, and jointly decided that she should at least drive back with Tammy to the site where the training took place. If she couldn't manage it, she could stay in the car until the course finished. En route, her courage returned. When she received her certificate, everyone else enrolled stood and applauded.

Then her right ankle disintegrated. Her doctors wanted to fuse the large affected bones into one piece. But that would have caused the other, smaller bones in her foot—now facing additional pressure—to deteriorate. That's not so intolerable, perhaps, when you're eighty (although it's no picnic then either). But it's no solution when you're in your teens. We insisted upon an artificial replacement, although the technology was new. There was a three year-waiting list. This was simply not manageable. The damaged ankle produced much more pain than her previously failing hip. One bad night she became erratic and illogical. I couldn't calm her down. I knew she was at her breaking point. To call that stressful is to say almost nothing.

We spent weeks and then months desperately investigating all sorts of replacement devices, trying to assess their suitability. We looked everywhere for quicker surgery: India, China, Spain, the UK, Costa Rica, Florida. We contacted the Ontario Provincial Ministry of Health. They were very helpful. They located a specialist across the country, in Vancouver. Mikhaila's ankle was replaced in November. Post-surgery, she was in absolute agony. Her foot was mispositioned. The cast was compressing skin against bone. The clinic was unwilling to give her enough oxycontin to control her pain. She had built up a high level of tolerance because of her previous use.

When she returned home, in less pain, Mikhaila started to taper off the opiates. She hated oxycontin, despite its evident utility. She said it turned her life grey. Perhaps that was a good thing, under the circumstances. She stopped using it as soon as possible. She suffered through withdrawal for months, with night sweating and formication (the sensation of ants crawling upside down under her skin). She became unable to experience any pleasure. That was another effect of opiate withdrawal.

During much of this period, we were overwhelmed. The demands of everyday life don't stop, just because you have been laid low by a catastrophe. Everything that you always do still has to be done. So how do you manage? Here are some things we learned:

Set aside some time to talk and to think about the illness or other crisis and how it should be managed every day. *Do not* talk or think about it otherwise. If you do not limit its effect, you will become exhausted, and everything will spiral into the ground. This is not helpful. Conserve your strength. You're in a war, not a battle, and a war is composed of many battles. You must stay functional through all of them. When worries associated with the crisis arise at other times, remind yourself that you will think them through, during the scheduled period. This usually works. The parts of your brain that generate anxiety are more interested in the fact that there is a plan than in the details of the plan. Don't schedule your time to think in the evening or at night. Then you won't be able to sleep. If you can't sleep, then everything will go rapidly downhill.

Shift the unit of time you use to frame your life. When the sun is shining, and times are good, and the crops are bountiful, you can make your plans for the next month, and the next year, and the next five years. You can even dream a decade ahead. But you can't do that when your leg is clamped firmly in a crocodile's jaws. "Sufficient unto the day are the evils thereof"—that is Matthew 6:34. It is often interpreted as "live in the present, without a care for tomorrow." This is not what it means. That injunction must be interpreted in the context of the Sermon on the Mount, of which it is an integral part. That sermon distills the ten "Thou-shalt-nots" of the Commandments of Moses into a single prescriptive "Thou shalt." Christ enjoins His followers to place faith in God's Heavenly Kingdom, and the truth. That's a conscious decision to presume the primary goodness of Being. That's an act of courage. Aim high, like Pinocchio's Geppetto. Wish upon a star, and then act properly, in accordance with that aim. Once you are aligned with the heavens, you can concentrate on the day. Be careful. Put the things you can control in order. Repair what is in disorder, and make what is already good better. It is possible that you can manage, if you are careful. People are very tough.

People can survive through much pain and loss. But to persevere they must see the good in Being. If they lose that, they are truly lost.

Dogs, Again—But Finally, Cats

Dogs are like people. They are the friends and allies of human beings. They are social, hierarchical, and domesticated. They are happy at the bottom of the family pyramid. They pay for the attention they receive with loyalty, admiration, and love. Dogs are great.

Cats, however, are their own creatures. They aren't social or hierarchical (except in passing). They are only semi-domesticated. They don't do tricks. They are friendly on their own terms. Dogs have been tamed, but cats have made a decision. They appear willing to interact with people, for some strange reasons of their own. To me, cats are a manifestation of nature, of Being, in an almost pure form. Furthermore, they are a form of Being that looks at human beings and approves.

When you meet a cat on a street, many things can happen. If I see a cat at a distance, for example, the evil part of me wants to startle it with a loud pfft! sound—front teeth over bottom lip. That will make a nervous cat puff up its fur and stand sideways so it looks larger. Maybe I shouldn't laugh at cats, but it's hard to resist. The fact that they can be startled is one of the best things about them (along with the fact that they are instantly disgruntled and embarrassed by their overreaction). But when I have myself under proper control, I'll bend down, and call the cat over, so I can pet it. Sometimes, it will run away. Sometimes, it will ignore me completely, because it's a cat. But sometimes the cat will come over to me, push its head against my waiting hand, and be pleased about it. Sometimes it will even roll over, and arch its back against the dusty concrete (although cats positioned in that manner will often bite and claw even a friendly hand).

Across the street on which I live is a cat named Ginger. Ginger is a Siamese, a beautiful cat, very calm and self-possessed. She is low in the Big Five personality trait of neuroticism, which is an index of anxiety, fear and emotional pain. Ginger is not at all bothered by dogs. Our dog, Sikko, is her friend. Sometimes when you call her—sometimes of her own accord—Ginger will trot across the street, tail held high, with a little kink at the end. Then she will roll on her back in front of Sikko, who wags his tail happily as a consequence. Afterward, if she feels like it, she might come visit you, for a half a minute. It's a nice break. It's a little extra light, on a good day, and a tiny respite, on a bad day.

If you pay careful attention, even on a bad day, you may be fortunate enough to be confronted with small opportunities of just that sort. Maybe you will see a little girl dancing on the street because she is all dressed up in a ballet costume. Maybe you will have a particularly good cup of coffee in a café that cares about their customers. Maybe you can steal ten or twenty minutes to do some little ridiculous thing that distracts you or reminds you that you can laugh at the absurdity of existence. Personally, I like to watch a *Simpsons* episode at 1.5 times regular speed: all the laughs; two-thirds the time.

And maybe when you are going for a walk and your head is spinning a cat will show up and if you pay attention to it then you will get a reminder for just fifteen seconds that the wonder of Being might make up for the ineradicable suffering that accompanies it.

Pet a cat when you encounter one on the street.

P.S. Soon after I wrote this chapter, Mikhaila's surgeon told her that her artificial ankle would have to be removed, and her ankle fused. Amputation waited down that road. She had been in pain for eight years, since the replacement surgery, and her mobility remained significantly impaired, although both were much better than before. Four days later she happened upon a new physiotherapist. He was a large, powerful, attentive person. He had specialized in ankle treatment in the UK, in London. He placed his hands around her ankle and compressed it for forty seconds, while Mikhaila moved her foot back and forth. A mispositioned bone slipped back where it belonged. Her pain disappeared. She never cries in front of medical personnel, but she burst into tears. Her knee straightened up. Now she can walk long distances, and traipse around in her bare feet. The calf muscle on her damaged leg is growing back. She has much more flexion in the artificial joint. This year, she got married and had a baby girl, Elizabeth, named after my wife's departed mother.

Things are good.

For now.

Coda

WHAT SHALL I DO WITH MY NEWFOUND PEN OF LIGHT?

In late 2016 I travelled to northern California to meet a friend and business associate. We spent an evening together thinking and talking. At one point he took a pen from his jacket and took a few notes. It was LED-equipped and beamed light out its tip, so that writing in the dark was made easier. "Just another gadget," I thought. Later, however, in a more metaphorical frame of mind, I was struck quite deeply by the idea of a pen of light. There was something symbolic about it, something metaphysical. We're all in the dark, after all, much of the time. We could all use something written with light to guide us along our way. I told him I wanted to do some writing, while we sat and conversed, and I asked him if he would give me the pen, as a gift. When he handed it over, I found myself inordinately pleased. Now I could write illuminated words in the darkness! Obviously, it was important to do such a thing properly. So I said to myself, in all seriousness, "What shall I do with my newfound pen of light?" There are two verses in the New Testament that pertain to such things. I've thought about them a lot:

> Ask, and it shall given to you; Seek, and ye shall find; Knock, and it shall be open unto you: For everyone who asks receives; the one who seeks finds; and to the one who knocks, the door will be opened (Matthew 7:7-7:8)

At first glance, this seems like nothing but a testament to the magic of prayer, in the sense of entreating God to grant favours. But God, whatever or whoever He may be, is no simple granter of wishes. When tempted by the Devil himself, in the desert—as we saw in Rule 7 (Pursue what is meaningful [not what is expedient])—even Christ Himself was not willing to call upon his Father for a favour; furthermore, every day, the prayers of desperate people go unanswered. But maybe this is because the questions they contain are not phrased in the proper manner. Perhaps it's not reasonable to ask God to break the rules of physics every time we fall by the wayside or make a serious error. Perhaps, in such times, you can't put the cart before the horse and simply wish for your problem to be solved in some magical manner. Perhaps you could ask, instead, what you might have to do right now to increase your resolve, buttress your character, and find the strength to go on. Perhaps you could instead ask to see the truth.

On many occasions in our nearly thirty years of marriage my wife and I have had a disagreement—sometimes a deep disagreement. Our unity appeared to be broken, at some unknowably profound level, and we were not able to easily resolve the rupture by talking. We became trapped, instead, in emotional, angry and anxious argument. We agreed that when such circumstances arose we would separate, briefly: she to one room, me to another. This was often quite difficult, because it is hard to disengage in the heat of an argument, when anger generates the desire to defeat and win. But it seemed better than risking the consequences of a dispute that threatened to spiral out of control.

Alone, trying to calm down, we would each ask ourselves the same single question: *What had we each done to contribute to the situation we were arguing about? However small, however distant … we had each made some error.* Then we would reunite, and share the results of our questioning: *Here's how I was wrong ….*

The problem with asking yourself such a question is that you must truly want the answer. And the problem with doing that is that *you won't like the answer.* When you are arguing with someone, you want to be right, and you want the other person to be wrong. Then it's them that has to sacrifice something and change, not you, and that's much preferable. If it's you that's wrong and you that must change, then you have to reconsider yourself—your memories of the past, your manner of being in the present, and your plans for the future. Then you must resolve to improve and figure out how to do that. Then you actually have to do it. That's exhausting. It takes repeated practice, to instantiate the new perceptions and make the new actions habitual. It's much easier just not to realize, admit and engage. It's much easier to turn your attention away from the truth and remain wilfully blind.

But it's at such a point that you must decide whether you want to be right or you want to have peace.[216] You must decide whether to insist upon the absolute correctness of your view, or to listen and negotiate. You don't get peace by being right. You just get to be right, while your partner gets to be wrong—defeated and wrong. Do that ten thousand times and your marriage will be over (or you will wish it was). To choose the alternative—to seek peace—you have to decide that you want the answer, more than you want to be right. That's the way out of the prison of your stubborn preconceptions. That's the prerequisite for negotiation. That's to truly abide by principle of Rule 2 (Treat yourself like someone you are responsible for helping).

My wife and I learned that if you ask yourself such a question, and you genuinely desire the answer (no matter how disgraceful and terrible and shameful), then a memory of something you did that was stupid and wrong at some point in the generally not-distant-enough past will arise from the depths of your mind. Then you can go back to your partner and reveal why you're an idiot, and apologize (sincerely) and that person can do the same for you, and then apologize (sincerely), and then you two idiots will be able to talk again. Perhaps that is true prayer: the question, "What have I done wrong, and what can I do now to set things at least a little bit more right?" But your heart must be open to the terrible truth. You must be receptive to that which you do not want to hear. When you decide to learn about your faults, so that they can be rectified, you open a line of communication with the source of all revelatory thought. Maybe that's the same thing as consulting your conscience. Maybe that's the same thing, in some manner, as a discussion with God.

It was in that spirit, with some paper in front of me, that I asked my question: *What shall I do with my newfound pen of light?* I asked, as if I truly wanted the answer. I waited for a reply. I was holding a conversation between two different elements of myself. I was genuinely thinking—or listening, in the sense described in Rule 9 (Assume that the person you are listening to might know something you don't). That rule can apply as much to yourself as to others. It was me, of course, who asked the question—and it was me, of course, who replied. But those two me's were not the same. I did not know what the answer would be. I was waiting for it to appear in the theatre of my imagination. I was waiting for the words to spring out of the void. How can a person think up something that surprises him? How can he already not know what he thinks? Where do new thoughts come from? Who or what thinks them?

Since I had just been given, of all things, a Pen of Light, which could write Illuminated Words in the darkness, I wanted to do the best thing I could with it. So, I asked the appropriate question—and, almost immediately, an answer

revealed itself: *Write down the words you want inscribed on your soul.* I
wrote that down. That seemed pretty good—a little on the romantic side,
granted—but that was in keeping with the game. Then I upped the ante. I
decided to ask myself the hardest questions I could think up, and await their
answers. If you have a Pen of Light, after all, you should use it to answer
Difficult Questions. Here was the first: *What shall I do tomorrow?* The
answer came: *The most good possible in the shortest period of time.* That was
satisfying, as well—conjoining an ambitious aim with the demands of
maximal efficiency. A worthy challenge. The second question was in the
same vein: *What shall I do next year? Try to ensure that the good I do then
will be exceeded only by the good I do the year after that.* That seemed solid,
too—a nice extension of the ambitions detailed in the previous answer. I told
my friend that I was trying a serious experiment in writing with the pen he
had given to me. I asked if I could read aloud what I had composed so far.
The questions—and the answers—struck a chord with him, too. That was
good. That was impetus to continue.

The next question ended the first set: *What shall I do with my life? Aim for
Paradise, and concentrate on today.* Hah! I knew what that meant. It's what
Geppetto does in the Disney movie *Pinocchio,* when he wishes upon a star.
The grandfatherly woodcarver lifts up his eyes to the twinkling diamond set
high above the mundane world of day-to-day human concerns and articulates
his deepest desire: that the marionette he created lose the strings by which he
is manipulated by others and transform himself into a real boy. It's also the
central message of the Sermon on the Mount, as we saw in Rule 4 (Compare
yourself to who you were yesterday …), but which deserve repeating here:

> And why take ye thought for raiment? Consider the lilies of the field, how they grow; they
> toil not, neither do they spin: And yet I say unto you, That even Solomon in all his glory
> was not arrayed like one of these. Wherefore, if God so clothe the grass of the field, which
> to day is, and to morrow is cast into the oven, shall he not much more clothe you, O ye of
> little faith? Therefore take no thought, saying, What shall we eat? or, What shall we drink?
> or, Wherewithal shall we be clothed? For your heavenly Father knoweth that ye have need
> of all these things. But seek ye first the kingdom of God, and his righteousness; and all
> these things shall be added unto you (Matthew 6:28-6:33).

What does all that mean? Orient yourself properly. Then—and only then—
concentrate on the day. Set your sights at the Good, the Beautiful, and the
True, and then focus pointedly and carefully on the concerns of each
moment. Aim continually at Heaven while you work diligently on Earth.

Attend fully to the future, in that manner, while attending fully to the present. Then you have the best chance of perfecting both.

I turned, then, from the use of time to my relationships with people, and wrote down and then read these questions and answers to my friend: *What shall I do with my wife? Treat her as if she is the Holy Mother of God, so that she may give birth to the world-redeeming hero. What shall I do with my daughter? Stand behind her, listen to her, guard her, train her mind, and let her know it's OK if she wants to be a mother. What shall I do with my parents? Act such that your actions justify the suffering they endured. What shall I do with my son? Encourage him to be a true Son of God.*

To honour your wife as a Mother of God is to notice and support the sacred element of her role as mother (not just of your children, but as such). A society that forgets this cannot survive. Hitler's mother gave birth to Hitler, and Stalin's mother to Stalin. Was something amiss in their crucial relationships? It seems likely, given the importance of the maternal role in establishing trust[217]—to take a single vital example. Perhaps the importance of their motherly duties, and of their relationship with their children, was not properly stressed; perhaps what the women were doing in their maternal guise was not properly regarded by husband, father and society alike. Who instead might a woman produce if she was treated properly, honourably and carefully? After all, the fate of the world rests on each new infant—tiny, fragile and threatened but, in time, capable of uttering the words and doing the deeds that maintain the eternal, delicate balance between chaos and order.

To stand behind my daughter? That's to encourage her, in everything she wants courageously to do, but to include in that genuine appreciation for the fact of her femininity: to recognize the importance of having a family and children and to forego the temptation to denigrate or devalue that in comparison to accomplishment of personal ambition or career. It's not for nothing that the Holy Mother and Infant is a divine image—as we just discussed. Societies that cease to honour that image—that cease to see that relationship as of transcendent and fundamental importance—also cease to be.

To act to justify the suffering of your parents is to remember all the sacrifices that all the others who lived before you (not least your parents) have made for you in all the course of the terrible past, to be grateful for all the progress that has been thereby made, and then to act in accordance with that remembrance and gratitude. People sacrificed immensely to bring about what we have now. In many cases, they literally died for it—and we should act with some respect for that fact.

To encourage my son to be a true Son of God? That is to want him above all *to do what is right,* and to strive to have his back while he is doing so. That is, I think, part of the sacrificial message: to value and support your son's commitment to transcendent good above all things (including his worldly progress, so to speak, and his safety—and, perhaps, even his life).

I continued asking questions. The answers came within seconds. *What shall I do with the stranger? Invite him into my house, and treat him like a brother, so that he may become one.* That's to extend the hand of trust to someone so that his or her best part can step forward and reciprocate. That's to manifest the sacred hospitality that makes life between those who do not yet know each other possible. *What shall I do with a fallen soul? Offer a genuine and cautious hand, but do not join it in the mire.* That's a good summary of what we covered in Rule 3 (Make friends with people who want the best for you). That's an injunction to refrain both from casting pearls before swine, and from camouflaging your vice with virtue. *What shall I do with the world? Conduct myself as if Being is more valuable than Non-Being.* Act so that you are not made bitter and corrupt by the tragedy of existence. That's the essence of Rule 1 (Stand up straight with your shoulders back): confront the uncertainty of the world voluntarily, and with faith and courage.

How shall I educate my people? Share with them those things I regard as truly important. That's Rule 8 (Tell the truth—or, at least, don't lie). That is to aim for wisdom, to distill that wisdom into words, and to speak forth those words as if they matter, with true concern and care. That's all relevant, as well, to the next question (and answer): *What shall I do with a torn nation? Stitch it back together with careful words of truth.* The importance of this injunction has, if anything, become clearer over the past few years: we are dividing, and polarizing, and drifting toward chaos. It is necessary, under such conditions, if we are to avoid catastrophe, for each of us to bring forward the truth, as we see it: not the arguments that justify our ideologies, not the machinations that further our ambitions, but the stark pure facts of our existence, revealed for others to see and contemplate, so that we can find common ground and proceed together.

What shall I do for God my Father? Sacrifice everything I hold dear to yet greater perfection. Let the deadwood burn off, so that new growth can prevail. That's the terrible lesson of Cain and Abel, detailed in the discussion of meaning surrounding Rule 7. *What shall I do with a lying man? Let him speak so that he may reveal himself.* Rule 9 (Listen …) is once again relevant here, as is another section of the New Testament:

> Ye shall know them by their fruits. Do men gather grapes of thorns, or figs of thistles? Even so every good tree bringeth forth good fruit; but a corrupt tree bringeth forth evil fruit. A good tree cannot bring forth evil fruit, neither can a corrupt tree bring forth good fruit. Every tree that bringeth not forth good fruit is hewn down, and cast into the fire. Wherefore by their fruits ye shall know them (Matthew 7:16-7:20).

The rot must be revealed before something sound can be put in its place, as was also indicated in Rule 7's elaboration—and all of this is pertinent to understanding the following question and answer: *How shall I deal with the enlightened one? Replace him with the true seeker of enlightenment.* There is no enlightened one. There is only the one who is seeking further enlightenment. Proper Being is process, not a state; a journey, not a destination. It's the continual transformation of what you know, through encounter with what you don't know, rather than the desperate clinging to the certainty that is eternally insufficient in any case. That accounts for the importance of Rule 4 (Compare yourself …). Always place your becoming above your current being. That means it is necessary to recognize and accept your insufficiency, so that it can be continually rectified. That's painful, certainly—but it's a good deal.

The next few Q & A's made another coherent group, focused this time on ingratitude: *What shall I do when I despise what I have? Remember those who have nothing and strive to be grateful.* Take stock of what is right in front of you. Consider Rule 12—somewhat tongue-in-cheek—(Pet a cat when you encounter one on the street). Consider, as well, that you may be blocked in your progress not because you lack opportunity, but because you have been too arrogant to make full use of what already lies in front of you. That's Rule 6 (Set your house in perfect order before you criticize the world).

I spoke recently with a young man about such things. He had barely ever left his family and never his home state—but he journeyed to Toronto to attend one of my lectures and to meet with me at my home. He had isolated himself far too severely in the short course of his life to date and was badly plagued by anxiety. When we first met, he could hardly speak. He had nonetheless determined in the last year to do something about all of that. He started by taking on the lowly job of dishwasher. He decided to do it well, when he could have treated it contemptuously. Intelligent enough to be embittered by a world that did not recognize his gifts, he decided instead to accept with the genuine humility that is the true precursor to wisdom whatever opportunity he could find. Now he lives on his own. That's better than living at home. Now he has some money. Not much. But more than none. And he earned it. Now he is confronting the social world, and benefitting from the ensuing conflict:

> *Knowledge frequently results*
> *from knowing others,*
> *but the man who is awakened,*
> *has seen the uncarved block.*
> *Others might be mastered by force,*
> *but to master one's self*
> *requires the Tao.*
> *He who has many material things,*
> *may be described as rich,*
> *but he who knows he has enough,*
> *and is at one with the Tao,*
> *might have enough of material things*
> *and have self-being as well.*[218]

As long as my still-anxious but self-transforming and determined visitor continues down his current path, he will become far more competent and accomplished, and it won't take long. But this will only be because he accepted his lowly state and was sufficiently grateful to take the first equally lowly step away from it. That's far preferable to waiting, endlessly, for the magical arrival of Godot. That's far preferable to arrogant, static, unchanging existence, while the demons of rage, resentment and unlived life gather around.

What shall I do when greed consumes me? Remember that it is truly better to give than to receive. The world is a forum of sharing and trading (that's Rule 7, again), not a treasure-house for the plundering. To give is to do what you can to make things better. The good in people will respond to that, and support it, and imitate it, and multiply it, and return it, and foster it, so that everything improves and moves forward.

What shall I do when I ruin my rivers? Seek for the living water and let it cleanse the Earth. I found this question, as well as its answer, particularly unexpected. It seems most associated with Rule 6 (Set your house …). Perhaps our environmental problems are not best construed technically. Maybe they're best considered psychologically. The more people sort themselves out, the more responsibility they will take for the world around them and the more problems they will solve.[219] It is better, proverbially, to rule your own spirit than to rule a city. It's easier to subdue an enemy without than one within. Maybe the environmental problem is ultimately spiritual. If we put ourselves in order, perhaps we will do the same for the world. Of course, what else would a psychologist think?

The next set were associated with proper response to crisis and exhaustion:

What shall I do when my enemy succeeds? Aim a little higher and be grateful for the lesson. Back to Matthew: "Ye have heard that it hath been said, Thou shalt love thy neighbour, and hate thine enemy. But I say unto you, Love your enemies, bless them that curse you, do good to them that hate you, and pray for them which despitefully use you, and persecute you; That ye may be the children of your Father which is in heaven" (5:43-5:45). What does this mean? Learn, from the success of your enemies; listen (Rule 9) to their critique, so that you can glean from their opposition whatever fragments of wisdom you might incorporate, to your betterment; adopt as your ambition the creation of a world in which those who work against you see the light and wake up and succeed, so that the better at which you are aiming can encompass them, too.

What shall I do when I'm tired and impatient? Gratefully accept an outstretched helping hand. This is something with a twofold meaning. It's an injunction, first, to note the reality of the limitations of individual being and, second, to accept and be thankful for the support of others—family, friends, acquaintances and strangers alike. Exhaustion and impatience are inevitable. There is too much to be done and too little time in which to do it. But we don't have to strive alone, and there is nothing but good in distributing the responsibilities, cooperating in the efforts, and sharing credit for the productive and meaningful work thereby undertaken.

What shall I do with the fact of aging? Replace the potential of my youth with the accomplishments of my maturity. This hearkens back to the discussion of friendship surrounding Rule 3, and the story of Socrates' trial and death—which might be summarized, as follows: *A life lived thoroughly justifies its own limitations.* The young man with nothing has his possibilities to set against the accomplishments of his elders. It's not clear that it's necessarily a bad deal, for either. "An aged man is but a paltry thing," wrote William Butler Yeats, "A tattered coat upon a stick, unless/Soul clap its hands and sing, and louder sing/For every tatter in its mortal dress ...."[220]

What shall I do with my infant's death? Hold my other loved ones and heal their pain. It is necessary to be strong in the face of death, because death is intrinsic to life. It is for this reason that I tell my students: aim to be the person at your father's funeral that everyone, in their grief and misery, can rely on. There's a worthy and noble ambition: strength in the face of adversity. That is very different from the wish for a life free of trouble.

What shall I do in the next dire moment? Focus my attention on the next right move. The flood is coming. The flood is always coming. The apocalypse is always upon us. That's why the story of Noah is archetypal. Things fall apart—we stressed that in the discussion surrounding Rule 10 (Be precise in your speech)—and the centre cannot hold. When everything has become chaotic and uncertain, all that remains to guide you might be the character you constructed, previously, by aiming up and concentrating on the moment at hand. If you have failed in that, you will fail in the moment of crisis, and then God help you.

That last set contained what I thought were the most difficult of all the questions I asked that night. The death of a child is, perhaps, the worst of catastrophes. Many relationships fail in the aftermath of such a tragedy. But dissolution in the face of such horror is not inevitable, although it is understandable. I have seen people immensely strengthen their remaining family bonds when someone close to them has died. I have seen them turn to those who remained and redouble their efforts to connect with them and support them. Because of that, all regained at least some of what had been so terribly torn away by death. We must therefore commiserate in our grief. We must come together in the face of the tragedy of existence. Our families can be the living room with the fireplace that is cozy and welcoming and warm while the storms of winter rage outside.

The heightened knowledge of fragility and mortality produced by death can terrify, embitter and separate. It can also awaken. It can remind those who grieve not to take the people who love them for granted. Once I did some chilling calculations regarding my parents, who are in their eighties. It was an example of the hated arithmetic we encountered in the discussion of Rule 5 (Do not let your children do anything that makes you dislike them)—and I walked through the equations so that I would stay properly conscious. I see my Mom and Dad about twice a year. We generally spend several weeks together. We talk on the phone in the interim between visits. But the life expectancy of people in their eighties is under ten years. That means I am likely to see my parents, if I am fortunate, fewer than twenty more times. That's a terrible thing to know. But knowing it puts a stop to my taking those opportunities for granted.

The next set of questions—and answers—had to do with the development of character. *What shall I say to a faithless brother? The King of the Damned is a poor judge of Being.* It is my firm belief that the best way to fix the world—a handyman's dream, if ever there was one—is to fix yourself, as we discussed in Rule 6. Anything else is presumptuous. Anything else risks harm, stemming from your ignorance and lack of skill. But that's OK. There's plenty to do, right where you are. After all, your specific personal faults detrimentally affect the world. Your conscious, voluntary sins (because no other word really works) makes things worse than they have to be. Your inaction, inertia and cynicism removes from the world that part of you that could learn to quell suffering and make peace. That's not good. There are endless reasons to despair of the world, and to become angry and resentful and to seek revenge.

Failure to make the proper sacrifices, failure to reveal yourself, failure to live and tell the truth—all that weakens you. In that weakened state, you will be unable to thrive in the world, and you will be of no benefit to yourself or to others. You will fail and suffer, stupidly. That will corrupt your soul. How could it be otherwise? Life is hard enough when it is going well. But when it's going badly? And I have learned through painful experience that nothing is going so badly that it can't be made worse. This is why Hell is a bottomless pit. This is why Hell is associated with that aforementioned sin. In the most awful of cases, the terrible suffering of unfortunate souls becomes attributable, by their own judgment, to mistakes they made knowingly in the past: acts of betrayal, deception, cruelty, carelessness, cowardice and, most commonly of all, willful blindness. To suffer terribly and to know yourself as the cause: that is Hell. And once in Hell it is very easy to curse Being itself. And no wonder. But it's not justifiable. *And that's why the King of the Damned is a poor judge of Being.*

How do you build yourself into someone on whom you can rely, in the best of times and the worst—in peace and in war? How do you build for yourself the kind of character that will not ally itself, in its suffering and misery, with all who dwell in Hell? The questions and answers continued, all pertinent, in one way or another, to the rules I have outlined in this book:

What shall I do to strengthen my spirit? Do not tell lies, or do what you despise.

What shall I do to ennoble my body? Use it only in the service of my soul.

What shall I do with the most difficult of questions? Consider them the gateway to the path of life.

What shall I do with the poor man's plight? Strive through right example to lift his broken heart.

What shall I do when the great crowd beckons? Stand tall and utter my broken truths.

And that was that. I still have my Pen of Light. I haven't written anything with it since. Maybe I will again when the mood strikes and something wells up from deep below. But, even if I don't, it helped me find the words to properly close this book.

I hope that my writing has proved useful to you. I hope it revealed things you knew that you did not know you knew. I hope the ancient wisdom I discussed provides you with strength. I hope it brightened the spark within you. I hope you can straighten up, sort out your family, and bring peace and prosperity to your community. I hope, in accordance with Rule 11 (Do not bother children when they are skateboarding), that you strengthen and encourage those who are committed to your care instead of protecting them to the point of weakness.

I wish you all the best, and hope that you can wish the best for others.

What will you write with your pen of light?